HAUNTED SAVANNAH

HAUNTED SAVANNAH

The Official Guidebook to Savannah Haunted History Tour

conducted by
Cobblestone Tours, Inc.

by James Caskey

BONAVENTTURE
books
SAVANNAH

Bonaventture Books
4602 Sussex Place
Savannah, GA 31405
Tel/ Fax: (912) 355- 7054
www.Bonaventture.com
Sales@Bonaventture.com

Photos are unadulterated originals, courtesy of James Caskey, and:

Georgia Historical Society, page 57

Craig Biszick, pages 93 and 94

Elizabeth Walker, page 112

Cristina Piva, page 116

Brian Caskey, page 124

Library of Congress Control Number 2005925067

Caskey, James. Haunted Savannah, The Official Guidebook to Savannah History Tour, conducted by Cobblestone Tours, Inc.

ISBN 0-9724224-2-0

ISBN 13: 978-0-972-4224-2-0

Sixth Edition, January 2011

Printed in Canada

ACKNOWLEDGMENTS

I have far too many people to thank for their time, patience and technical expertise to list in this volume. I've interviewed historians, authors, tour guides, and many people who work at the establishments mentioned within these pages. Without their help, this book would not have been possible. Any inaccuracies, errors of fact, or omissions contained within this volume are my own.

Unfortunately I can't acknowledge everyone by name, but a short list is possible. Local historian Becky Clark gave her time, provided a substantial amount of great material, and spent a good deal of time correcting the minutiae of Savannah's history contained in these pages. Historian Colin Young also gave his time freely and cheerfully—you have my thanks. Jewell Anderson & the staff at the Georgia Historical Society provided an incredible amount of patience with this amateur researcher—thanks for all your help. Tour guide and amateur historian Missy Brandt provided several anecdotes, but fortunately she allowed me to pay her off with sushi. Laura Lukasik kept me working with her boundless enthusiasm.

But a special thanks goes out to my mother, who has always been an inspiration to me because of her strength, and to my brother Brian, who in our childhood bought me my first book that was mine and mine alone: *The Horse that Played Centerfield.*

CONTENTS

Introduction: Savannah - Why So Haunted?

"The past is never dead. It's not even past."

—William Faulkner
Act I, Scene III, *Requiem for a Nun*

One cannot walk down Savannah's streets at twilight without feeling evidence of her supernatural side. The old beautiful homes practically emanate the aura of lost loves, lives cut short, and other misfortunes. The Spanish moss-drenched live oaks set the mood. The dead never truly depart in Savannah. One just has to walk into a shop, hotel or restaurant in Savannah and strike up a conversation with the staff, and the talk will turn inevitably to the supernatural. Any old tavern worth its salt has a good ghost story. It is in these stories we find common elements: tragedy, lost youth, and occasionally, redemption. Can a better setting for a ghost story be found than the Olde Pink House, or the Kehoe House? Savannah's Historic District sets the mood like no other city.

One of the theories regarding Savannah's prominence in all realms haunted has to do with energy. There is speculation that houses could possibly store a 'dry charge' of the energy expended in the structure, much like a battery can store electrical power. This energy could be bound to the property by moments of extreme emotional distress by the inhabitants, such as death or great sadness. There is also the possibility that an action repeated over and over again can also have this effect, which would explain why hearing footsteps is one of the most common forms of a structure being haunted. From time to time, when conditions are right, that stored power is unleashed. An analogy would be with sound waves: energy is released in audible form, and when conditions allow, such as an object bouncing the sound waves back toward the point of origin, the energy returns in the form of an echo. If energy can bounce back and return in this way several seconds after the actual event, why can't psychic energy return at a later time as well? And if an echo can return several seconds after the event, could it be possible that the psychic energy could return years, decades or even centuries after the fact? So ghosts may be an explainable phenomenon in this way. The lack of scientific proof of the existence of ghosts may be that we have thus far been unable to duplicate the conditions under which such an event might occur, or perhaps science has not developed the technology to record this psychic energy.

There is also another factor to consider: many old port cities have a reputation for being haunted. Seaports such as Charleston, Savannah, Wilmington, and New Orleans have garnered the reputation of having many supernatural occurrences. Perhaps it is tied in with the close proximity to the oceans and rivers—if ghosts are life-force energy that has not faded away, then maybe the tidal action and ebb and flow of the water has somehow polarized the entire area, preserving the remaining energy and capturing it for a time when conditions are right.

⋘ Types of Hauntings ⋙

Supernatural activity may be defined by the type of occurrences observed or experienced. Some take the form of what is known as a 'residual haunting', such as hearing footsteps in a deserted hallway or seeing a brief glimpse of someone or something which disappears. Residual hauntings can be audible, visible or even olfactory, such as smelling pipe tobacco when no one in the house is smoking. If the residual energy is visible, the incident is often referred to as a 'spectre' or an 'apparition'. Spectres or apparitions differ from true ghosts because there is no true interaction with the living. Imagine an endless video loop, where instead of an image playing on a television there is instead an image or occurrence which 'plays' on this physical plane.

If any of the eyewitness accounts in the following pages are correct, there are also ghosts which can interact with the living. Ghostly loved ones who can appear— usually in the middle of the night— to deliver words of comfort to the living; ghosts known for locking or unlocking doors, or even moving or hiding objects are some of the occurrences noted.

Another form of haunting is a poltergeist, which is German for 'noisy ghost'. Poltergeists are not as easy to attribute to the spirit of a departed soul; a poltergeist more resembles pent-up energy which can create havoc in the area afflicted by such a phenomenon. Poltergeists frequently (but not always) are associated with households with adolescent children. A poltergeist can be playful, destructive, or downright terrifying.

✎ History is the Key ✎

If any of these theories regarding how or why hauntings occur is correct, then why is Savannah a nexus for such supernatural happenings? What causes her to experience psychic echoes with such regularity?

To understand why Savannah is so haunted, one must look at her history. She's endured several great fires, numerous Yellow Fever Epidemics, and has been involved in both the Revolutionary War and the War Between The States. Tragedy is her calling-card. The historical record is full of this Savannah mainstay: violent death tempered with an ironic spin. Savannah has a dark and twisted nature, and she certainly has a sense of humor.

So this link with tragic history may go a long way towards explaining exactly why Savannah is hailed as one of the most haunted cities in America. Certainly, the legacy goes all the way back to when the area was inhabited by Indians. In 1736, the local Native Americans told the eventual founder of Methodism, John Wesley, that they believed that the spirits of their fallen comrades persisted near where they fell or were buried. Also, the Native Americans claimed to hear strange noises near where they had burned prisoners (which was an Indian custom). Traditionally, Native Americans have been superstitious regarding the spirit world, and the idea that one's ancestors watch over the living is an idea which goes back thousands of years.

One more possible explanation is that there is such a strong Irish presence in Savannah. Skeptics might charge that one type of spirits begets another, but one cannot dismiss the strong storytelling tradition of the Irish people. The Great Potato Famine was ravaging the Irish at the same time that Savannah was booming with King Cotton, so a good number of transports full of refugees found their way to our shores, bringing their long history of oral traditions with them. The

Irish have a healthy respect for the supernatural, and their stories reflect that attitude.

Another ethnicity which is conducive to the traditional art of ghost storytelling is the Sea Island people, called the Ogeechee, Geechee (or mistakenly referred to as 'Gullah') people. This unique cultural phenomenon was so important that it was dedicated a whole chapter in this volume ('Slave & Geechee Culture').

Perhaps her special connection with history as well as the special ethnicities of Savannah and the surrounding areas (Indian, Irish, and African-American) can explain why Georgia's First City is forever associated with the supernatural. Strange historical happenings are the norm in Savannah. Consider these instances:

- Several bodies were discovered in 1967 when roadwork was done on Abercorn St., right next to Colonial Park Cemetery. Presumably the City pulled up the tombstones to make way for both a city street and sidewalk next to the burial ground in 1896.

- In 1915, a group of boys stole human bones from a burial site 5 miles north of the city. Turns out, they were the remains of Revolutionary War hero Gen. Samuel Elbert. The children gave the bones to the Georgia Historical Society, where the librarian placed them in a desk drawer for 9 years.

- In 1779, during the American Revolution, the Allied forces were repulsed by the British in a massive battle inside the current Historic District of Savannah. It was the single bloodiest hour of the Revolution. The casualties from this battle were estimated at 1,100 and were buried in a mass grave—the location of which is unknown even today.

Another strange occurrence in the early days of Savannah happened in 1820. That particular year is remembered as one of the worst in Savannah's history, with a great fire and a Yellow Fever epidemic. An embittered departing editor of a local paper, one John M. Harney, wrote a scathing poem as he left the city which placed a curse on Savannah. It ended with, *"I leave you, Savannah, a curse that is far/ The worst of all curses - to remain as you are!"* Perhaps Savannah is indeed cursed, but there are some who look at the wondrous old houses and buildings of the Historic District and muse that 'Harney's curse' may have preserved us, as well.

☙ The Fascination ☙

Explaining why ghosts exist or what their scientific cause may be does not ask the more important question: why do ghost stories fascinate us? Whether you are a believer or not is irrelevant—the fact remains that Savannah is a town which *believes* itself to be haunted. Why do we care? What part of our curiosity is being satisfied by the telling and retelling of ghost tales?

It is my belief that we are looking for a touchstone to the past. Living downtown, I see tourists wandering around in Colonial Park Cemetery, taking photos of tombstones with which they have no literal connection. But the truth of the matter is that there does in fact exist a correlation. In the old cemetery plot, we see ourselves, figuratively speaking. We as a society also are fascinated by antiques and old photographs. I believe we are looking for some sort of kinship with who or what was here before us. We want to feel as though we can make sense of who we are and where we are going and the way to get a feel for the direction is to know where we've been. Learning about history connects us, and that same history is Savannah's most precious resource.

It is important to point out that I do not consider myself a paranormal researcher, even though many of my own observations and experiences have been included. I also do not classify myself as even an amateur historian. I am simply a tour guide, and a history lover.

My first (and perhaps even my second) reaction to something strange or unusual is not to blame it on the spirits of the departed. I always look for a logical explanation. More often than not, that bump in the night is a balky water pipe that has slowly worked its way loose, and the phantom footstep is nothing more than the settlings of an old house. But Savannah has so many bizarre happenings on such a regular basis, that after a while you simply cannot deny any longer her special connection to the spirit world. I feel I did not choose this hobby so much as it chose me—as you will see in a few of the upcoming chapters.

☙ A Personal History ☙

My first introduction to what I would deem the paranormal happened when I was a young child. My family was at a restaurant in my hometown of DeLand, Florida, and my mother Helen was sitting with a very odd expression on her face. She couldn't seem to stop staring at a man across the room at another table. When asked if she was all right, she commented that she was fine but she had a very funny feeling about the man, who in all respects appeared normal. She even described a dark veil descending around him. I remember that my mother endured some good-natured teasing about blatantly staring at this poor diner in the restaurant. But the teasing abruptly stopped when halfway through the meal, the man suddenly flopped out of his chair. He had dropped dead of a heart attack literally in mid-bite. Needless to say, this had an impression on me at that early age.

Even so, when I moved to Savannah I would have still classified myself as a skeptic when it came to ghosts. I have had that attitude challenged over and over again, as first seen in the chapter labeled 'Ft. Screven Inn'. When people learn of my interest in the paranormal, they often are quickly telling their own ghost tale. It feels at times like a Catholic confession. Their stories usually start the same way: "You're going to think I'm crazy, but..." These same people seem comforted when I confirm that they are not alone—in fact it is my belief people as a general rule have at least one unexplainable (if not paranormal) incident in the course of life.

Names, when requested, have been omitted or changed. Likewise, addresses have been removed if requested. But otherwise these tales are exactly as told to me. The people described within these pages are real. These are their stories.

M oon River Brewing Company

On Bay St. between Bull & Whitaker Streets, there exists a beautiful example of early 19th century architecture, formerly known as the old City Hotel, built in 1821. Designed as a Regency Style hotel, the structure today exists as the Moon River Brewing Company, which is both a fine microbrewery as well as one of the city's better seafood restaurants. Moon River was featured on the Travel Channel program 'America's Most Haunted Places- Savannah'. Interviews with historians Colin Young and Rebecca Clark appear on the segment, as well as this author. I also led a tour group, including the film crew, through the upstairs of the abandoned former hotel.

The notable former home of the City Hotel is tied intimately to the history of the area in a number of different ways. The downstairs at one time leased space to both the Bank of the United States, and to the Postal Service. The City Hotel was visited by General Winfield Scott, the Marquis de Lafayette, and John James Audubon, who ended up staying almost six months after his boat was damaged in a storm. During the 1830's, the owner even had a pair of lions on display. Located on what was then the busiest street in Savannah, the bar and wine cellar quickly gained a good reputation amongst cultivated businessmen in Savannah society. The bar was a meeting place for young men who gambled in the early part of the 19th century, and often times the haze of alcohol coupled with the rising monetary losses would result in 'affairs of honor', or duels. So the City Hotel was connected to the social, commercial, political and moral condition of Savannah at that time.

In Savannah a duel during that time period was not fought Old West style: we were much more civilized about how we went about killing each other. There were rules about how a proper duel was conducted, called the Code Duello, or Duelist's Code. If a man felt his reputation was being assailed, he would issue a challenge to the offender in writing, a letter calling their potential adversary such things as a *scoundrel*, a *lying rascal* or a *scallywag*. This letter would be not only delivered to the challenged, but also nailed up around town for all to see, a custom known as 'posting'. A posting of a challenge might even be printed in the local paper. Also involved were the best friends of the two antagonizing parties. These best friends were known as 'seconds', who were assistants during the duel. These friends were important, because if the duelist was unable to fight the duel for whatever reason, the second could be called on to fight the duel in his place.

The duels often had their origin at the City Hotel bar, but often ended across the river on the Carolina shore because duels technically were illegal in Savannah. One affair of honor did originate at the City Hotel but never took place. A man with poor eyesight was challenged to a duel at the bar, and accepted. Under the Code, he was able to pick the location of the duel, so he announced that the duel would be fought at an unusual spot: the nearest convenient table next to the bar at the hotel. When the challenger questioned the choice of location, the man with poor eyesight pointed out that he was at a distinct disadvantage at ten or twenty paces since he was so nearsighted, and was simply making sure they had an equal footing. The challenger, seeing that the duel would kill them both, quickly apologized, and the planned duel was abruptly cancelled. The man with defective eyesight had won some hard-earned respect.

Bad Blood

But reconciliation was not the case in 1832. Two men had a disagreement, and this particular case was unusual because the affair of honor both began and ended at the City Hotel.

In the spring of 1832, James Jones Stark, who had a reputation for being a bit of a drunken braggart, expressed his dislike of local doctor Philip Minis, a well-liked member of one of the oldest families in Georgia. The language used in the insult was so vulgar that they cannot be recounted in this volume. The specific nature of their quarrel was not known, but Stark made it plain that he held a low regard for those of the Jewish persuasion, thus taking a shot at Dr. Minis' ancestry. In August, Dr. Minis, no longer able to let the matter simply pass as the ramblings of an anti-Semitic drunkard, demanded either an apology or "that satisfaction which one gentleman should afford another." When the two men could not agree on terms of the duel, Stark continued to ridicule Minis' courage. On August 10th, James Stark and a friend were coming down the stairs in the City Hotel just in time to hear Dr. Minis declare, "I proclaim James Stark a coward!" Stark put his hand in his pocket as if to draw a pistol, and advanced toward Minis, who drew his pistol and fired, killing Stark. Apparently Stark had more liquor in him than sense, because the pocket that he had menacingly reached into was empty.

Dr. Philip Minis was tried for murder, but the jury deliberated for just two hours before finding him innocent of all charges.

The City Hotel was used as a hospital by the Confederate forces during the War Between the States, and never reopened its doors as an active hotel after the war. Savannah's fortunes seemed tied to the old hotel: the cotton industry slowly entered a decline in the 20th century, and both the hotel and the downtown were left to molder and decay. The economy stagnated. Local industries such as paper mills and textile plants polluted the ecology—both the air and the river. Ship captains joked that they moored in Savannah to poison the barnacles off their hulls. In 1946, visitor Lady Astor said about Savannah: "Savannah is a beautiful lady with a dirty face." Several Savannah landmarks were lost—including Savannah's Union Station, which was bigger and grander than Grand Central Station in New York City. Many well-meaning developers did further damage by renovating historic structures incorrectly, such as the Savannah Theatre, built by William Jay, which now sports an Art Deco façade.

☜The Brewing Company Renovation ☞

The old former hotel spent most of the 20th century as storage space and an office supply. The structure and roof were damaged extensively in Hurricane David, in 1979. A new company bought the now-ruined edifice, and renovations were begun to turn the space into a bar, restaurant and brewery (originally titled "Oglethorpe Brewing Company") which opened in December of 1996. The initial concept was that the bar was going to be downstairs, and the upstairs was going to be a restaurant. However, the crew that tried to renovate the second floor reputedly ran into some difficulty of an otherworldly nature.

When the upstairs area was being renovated, the workers complained of problems with their electrical equipment. Some claimed to experience cold spots, a sensation of being watched, and some even complained of experiencing the sensation of being pushed, pinched, or tugged on their clothing. One worker claimed that something unseen had tried to trip him. The foreman of the job became convinced that the ghost was a female, and even named her, jokingly calling the strange spirit 'Mrs. Wilson'.

It was said the foreman's joking ended shortly thereafter. He had been willing to view the strange occurrences with good humor, but he had a big problem with Mrs. Wilson when she decided to attack his wife! It seems the wife of the foreman had come by the site to deliver his lunch, and on her way down the stairs leading to the first floor, she felt a sharp push in the back, and no one had been on the stairs behind her. The foreman is said to have tendered his resignation on the spot and left the property.

The work was called to a close on the upstairs, and the second floor is instead used as a storage area today. The first level serves as the bar and restaurant. The three floors above what became Moon River Brewing Company (it was re-christened and opened in 1999) remain largely untouched and unrenovated, with the majority of the beautiful early 19th century architecture intact, yet crumbling. Immense pocket doors, since removed from their wall slots can still be viewed on the second floor, as well as a curved door—giving clues to the opulence of the old hotel. Regency Style was a very desirable form of architecture, and several well-to-do Savannahians had their homes designed in that very style, a few of which still exist today.

Tour Occurrences

But the strange reputation of the building persists. Several haunted pub tours go into the unrenovated area, and several tourgoers and tour guides alike have claimed to have had some strange experiences, including this author. I myself have had unexplainable occurrences on more than one occasion.

On one cold evening, a man on the tour expressed to me his disbelief in all things supernatural. He even complained that his wife had cajoled him into taking a ghost tour, and he chose this particular tour because he could at least have a beer while his wife listened to the stories. After the story I tell in the upstairs of Moon River had concluded, we were walking back down the stairs to the first level. This gentleman was right in front of me as we descended, and suddenly he slapped his hand to the side of his neck and whirled around, looking at me suspiciously. He later admitted to me the reason for this bizarre behavior: he claimed to have felt a hand on his neck, which grabbed his scarf. He thought at first that it was me, reaching down and grabbing him, and that I was either playing a joke on him or perhaps even picking on him for publicly stating that he didn't believe in ghosts. But when he turned around behind me he suddenly realized that I had my hands full, and was *eight feet behind him.*

Another instance comes to mind. One night a young woman, after hearing the story and descending from the upper floor, asked me about the woman in period costume she had seen lurking in the shadows. My response? "What woman in period costume?" She had been convinced that it was part of the tour, and was disappointed when the woman disappeared into a room and had not reappeared.

Tour guide Karl Kessler has also had some strange instances. He has experienced a choking sensation while telling his tale on the second level, and also claimed to have once felt a sensation "like someone pouring ice-cold water down my back" as he was relating a story. In yet another happening, he was leaving the upper area with his group one evening and heard someone's footsteps walking in the central hallway behind him. Thinking that he had missed a member of his tour group, he went back to find them. The footsteps were indeed walking in the hallway, but no one was there. "It sounded like they walked right past me, and I felt a chill. I got the heck out of there."

A psychic who visited the upstairs grew incredibly cold to the touch and told a tale of a now-departed worker in the hotel, a woman who practiced voodoo. Could this be the 'Mrs. Wilson' of which the workers complained? This psychic also appeared to step around something unseen in her path in the upstairs of the former hotel, and when asked why she did so, she replied, "I'm sorry, I just thought it would be terribly rude to step right *through* them..."

One elderly tourgoer claimed to have received a stinging slap on her arm during the tour into the upstairs, and upon examination she did indeed have a red mark resembling a slap-mark. The next day her arm had a bruise which had the whole family talking—because the mark was on her right arm, and the bruise was in the shape of a right handprint.

⋞☙ The Staff's Experiences ☙⋟

Even some members of the staff are leery of going into areas of the Brewing Company. A bartender named Amanda claims that as she went into the upstairs, she felt a hand on her neck as she entered a main hallway. She whirled to confront what she assumed was a co-worker pulling a prank, but there was no one: she was all alone. Amanda also had a strange occurrence in the basement, when one night she went down the stairs alone. She saw a man out of the corner of her eye, and blinked, thinking that she was seeing things. The apparition did not vanish, however, and for several moments she and this spectre regarded each other before she finally slowly backed out of the area. She claims that he was wearing 19th century attire.

Another employee, a waiter named Sam, claims to have heard strange pounding and knocking sounds in the basement, near a large archway. The sound, he says, was distinctly that of someone knocking on a wooden door—but the downstairs archway's large wooden door has been removed years ago. Sam refuses to go into the basement alone at the end of the night anymore, a claim verified and echoed by several members of the wait staff.

The resident brewmaster, John, claims the bar is not haunted. He related some wonderful history of the structure to this author during an interview, but he claims to have never had any sort of paranormal experience at Moon River. "I've worked all night here, and never had any sort of haunting happen to me. Back in 2002, we had a group of paranormal researchers study this place, and they presented their findings to us in a large volume. I was looking forward to reading it to see what they found, but I was disappointed because I could easily explain away all of their experiences. For instance, they claimed that in one corner of the basement that they could smell vomit, and they were standing next to a grease vent."

John went on to say that he has tried to keep an open mind, but has been accused of being a close-minded skeptic. When it was pointed out to him that the origin of the word 'skeptic' means 'open-minded', and that the Greek root word literally means 'to examine', John smiled. "Exactly. I want to believe, or at least experience something I can't explain, but it hasn't happened to me yet."

If it is indeed haunted, there is one other ghost at Moon River, seemingly having found a home in the basement. Sometimes the beer taps downstairs will be found flipped open, and on a number of occasions this has caused a flood downstairs, not of water, but of gallons and gallons of precious beer. This has been known to happen even though the taps must be turned on by a key, and the lock is found in the 'off' position. Evidently the ghost which calls the basement home enjoys 'the spirits', as well.

The Moon River Brewing Company is located at 21 W. Bay St., and is Savannah's only operating microbrewery. Moon River serves both lunch & dinner. Large groups can call (912) 447-0943 for reserving table space, but reservations are not required for smaller parties.

L ittle Gracie

At the corner of Bryan and Bull Streets, a 1950's era structure sits on a very historic corner. The original tything lot (Oglethorpe's plan called for a series of residential plots built around the squares, which were known as tything lots) was where James Habersham, Sr. called his home in Savannah. Habersham was a planter, and also the headmaster of Bethesda Orphanage. But more importantly, the site also formerly housed the old Pulaski Hotel.

There is debate as to when the Pulaski Hotel was built, with some evidence that the hotel could have been built as far back as 1795. Others place it at a much more conservative 1835, but whatever the date the Pulaski Hotel was one of the finest hotels of the period. In the 1880's it came under new management: the Watson family, W. J. and Frances, originally from Boston by way of Charleston. The Watsons found themselves excluded and ostracized from Savannah society. Frances Watson wanted to fit into Savannah society, and she was a smart woman. She used the Hotel at her disposal. It's amazing how many new friends the Watsons had when they started giving away free food and drink, especially in a setting as fine as the Pulaski Hotel. Mrs. Watson only invited the Savannah elite, so in a matter of no time she was also considered a member of the Savannah elite as well.

Her daughter, little Gracie Watson, was born in 1883; she was also included in these parties. She was entertaining the guests by the age of three, and by the age of six was playing the role of hostess. She was much- loved by the Savannah elite. Gracie liked all the attention, and also liked helping her mother, but Gracie, her being a child at a party for adults, would become bored. Gracie would often slip away, and could be found playing underneath the back stairwell of the old Pulaski Hotel. In fact, it became a joke amongst the partygoers: when Gracie would disappear, they had overstayed their welcome. Someone would ask the question, "Where's Gracie? If Gracie has disappeared, it must be time for us to go as well." Gracie (or lack thereof) was a better indicator of the lateness of the hour than the clock on the old Exchange Building.

Gracie passed away two days before Easter in 1889 at the age of six, due to pneumonia. After her death, Gracie's mother claimed to be able to still hear little Gracie laughing and playing up underneath that stairwell. Many people thought that perhaps the strain of losing Gracie was proving to be too much for Mrs. Watson. It was especially upsetting for Mr. Watson. Her husband decided to move them both to the newly-opened DeSoto Hotel, to get her away from so many memories at the Pulaski. The family erected a life-sized statue of little Gracie out at Bonaventure Cemetery.

Over the years many staff members would claim to hear the sounds of a little girl laughing and playing when they got near that stairwell, but no little girl could be found. Other staff members refused to go into the basement of the old hotel, because of the moans heard occasionally, and the sound of clanking iron. The downstairs had at one time been used to store slaves who had been transported to the Americas from Africa— as was common with many buildings with basements near Bay St. The Pulaski Hotel was eventually torn down in 1957, and replaced with a cafeteria, which remained open   until the fall of 2001. The structure, fully renovated, is now a bank.

Many thought that the sights and sounds of Gracie would disappear when the Old Pulaski Hotel was demolished, but this has not proven to be the case. Beyond the last archway to the right if you were to face from Bull St. is where the back stairwell of the old Pulaski Hotel used to be located, roughly twenty-five feet down a hallway, where the ladies room was. The sounds of Little Gracie can still be heard, laughing and playing at this spot. People have reported seeing a small girl run past them in period dress, and when they turn to see where she is headed in such a hurry, no little girl can be seen. This ghost was even seen by fellow tour guide Reagan Howard, who glimpsed a little girl through the windows of the then-abandoned structure. So little Gracie to this day is still avoiding the party of the Savannah elite, slipping away and laughing and playing near that stairwell.

Former tour guide Naomi Starr had a strange experience involving the story of Gracie in the spring of 2002. She led her group to a convenient area across the street and was beginning her story, when she suddenly noticed that she could see a four-story building reflected in the window of the bank she was facing instead of the two-story former cafeteria. She turned around and faced the then-abandoned structure, but saw nothing out of the ordinary, but the reflection of a building she did not recognize remained in view for the entirety of her story. When she related the story to this author, I pulled out a photograph of the four-story Pulaski Hotel and showed it to her. Naomi went deathly pale, and after taking a moment to recover informed me that I was holding a picture of the building she had seen reflected.

Often, there are questions about why Gracie would come back to that location. After all, her parents are gone, and so is the original structure of the Pulaski Hotel. One possible answer is that the site was originally James Habersham's downtown home—as headmaster and teacher of orphans, it would stand to reason he might have quite a bit of experience guiding lost children. Perhaps Gracie has found comfort with this mentor presence.

☞A Friendly Spirit☜

This ghost story also has some personal significance. One night in early 2001, right as tour was beginning, this author had two women join the tour. One of them asked, "What can you tell me about the Piccadilly Cafeteria?" The question was so odd that I asked if she had had an experience there. She said yes, she had. I asked her if her experience had happened in the ladies room—and all the color drained from this woman's face. She grew increasingly pale as I told her the story of little Gracie. She then told me that right before tour, she and her friend had eaten at the Piccadilly, and (how to phrase this delicately?) had both drank a bit too much sweet tea. They went to the rest room, and when they were sitting down in their stalls, something unseen in the restroom pulled both of their pocketbooks out from under the stall door. In her words, she couldn't think of a better place to be sitting when something like that occurred! They both sprang up, thinking they were being robbed, but they found their purses lying in the center of the bathroom floor. Nothing was missing. Things had been pulled out, but not money. Lipstick, makeup and candy had been pulled out of both purses—items which would draw the interest of a little girl.

So little Gracie still laughs and plays in that area, and sometimes she invites a friend or two with which to play.

๛Erroneous Folklore๛

Gracie has a bit of folklore attached to her story, specifically referencing her statue in Bonaventure Cemetery. On the Fox Family television show "Scariest Places on Earth", the claim was made that the statue of Gracie pictured on the program was dedicated to a victim of Rene Rondolia, the supposed killer of children. This simply cannot be true, since the fictional Rene was supposedly killed by an angry mob in 1820, and Gracie died of pneumonia in 1889.

Amongst the many historical inaccuracies portrayed on that program (such as missing the correct date of the bombardment of Ft. Pulaski by a whole year), the statue was incorrectly identified as being located in Colonial Park Cemetery; the real location is Bonaventure, some four miles away. Also, a tunnel allegedly "used by Rene" was also misidentified as being located in Colonial Park. The tunnel's real location is in Forsyth Park.

A story was told that her statue would become warm and begin to cry when the "ghost of Rene" was near. Not only is the story false, but this author cannot stress enough that one should never, ever touch a statue, tombstone, or any type of funeral marker in a cemetery. Gracie's beautiful marker is now enclosed by a tall iron fence, designed by master iron worker Michael Sebacher, to keep people from trying to touch the statue. Anyone who touches or damages a burial marker in a cemetery will find themselves ejected from the burial ground, and possibly on the receiving end of criminal charges. One should take only memories and leave only prayers in cemeteries and graveyards.

Olde Pink House

On Reynolds Square, the Olde Pink House restaurant sits as both a standard for Southern cuisine and a wonderful example of 18th century Georgian architecture. It was originally the home of James

Habersham Jr. To tell James Jr.'s story is to tell the tale of so many Savannah families in the late 18th century: families divided over loyalty.

James Jr. was one of three sons of James Habersham Sr., who was a colonial planter and merchant, and one of the wealthiest men in the colony. It was James the Elder who sent the first bales of cotton from Georgia to England. He was also the headmaster of the school at Bethesda Orphanage, first orphanage in America, and a chief proponent of repeal of the ban on slavery. He was also a fierce Loyalist. He was in was nearing the end of his life as the first rumbles of Revolution began to be heard. Habersham Sr. was dismayed to find that all three of his sons were sympathetic to the Colonial cause, and they were involved with the Sons of Liberty. It broke his heart that his boys would fight against the Crown he had spent his life serving, and they would find themselves arrayed "father against son, and son against father."

James Jr. was a war hero during the Revolutionary War, attaining the rank of major in the Colonial forces. It was James Jr.'s elder brother, Joseph, who would achieve lasting fame, however, for what could be the boldest act of the Revolution. On January 18th, 1776, at the Governor's Mansion on Telfair Square, Joseph and a small group of men literally *walked* into the Governor's residence and arrested him. Joseph, aged 24 years, put his hand upon the shoulder of the man who was in theory the most powerful man in Georgia, and said, "Sir James, you are my prisoner."

The house itself was begun in 1771, and completed in 1789. The completion of the house was held up by the British occupation during the Revolutionary War. It was constructed out of red brick and then covered with white stucco, and it is said that the restaurant got its name when the red brick bled through the stucco and turned it pink. Keep in mind that James Habersham was a Colonial warrior, and he didn't want to be known as the war hero living in the big pink house on Reynolds Square, so he had it painted white. The white paint never did do an adequate job of covering the pink color up, as the bricks kept bleeding through the stucco and turning it pink yet again. Every so often, the house would turn pink. This continued until the 1920's, when a woman who ran the home as a tea room finally decided to paint it pink. Sometimes it does take a woman to think of something as sensible as painting the Olde Pink House a shade of pink.

↞One of America's Most Haunted ↠

The Travel Channel program 'America's Most Haunted Places-Savannah' featured the Olde Pink House, featuring both the upstairs and the lower tavern. One former waiter interviewed described a strange light appearing in the 'Purple Room' on the upper floor. He said that it appeared as a floating orb, raced around the room, and then vanished.

An instance involving candles occurred in one of the dining rooms. A waitress who blew out the tea lights in the center of each table found that they had been mysteriously re-lit when she stepped out of the room for a moment. She could even see the smoke still hovering in the air from where she had blown them out, but all the lights were re-lit. Another waitress reported trying to pull a tablecloth off a table at the end of an evening, and something pulled right back! She got into a tug- of- war with something unseen on the other end, *and lost*. She fled the room.

Another waitress reported seeing the apparition of a young woman dressed in servant's clothing from what appeared to be the early 19th century. So the modern server got a glimpse of the former server, and then the young girl retreated deferentially into the far north upstairs dining room. The waitress walked into the room to verify that there was someone in a costume in that room, and found nothing but empty tables. She described the woman as wearing a scarf on her head, and being "incredibly meek, and sad."

Although there have been many instances of strange happenings on the upper floors, many believe the downstairs tavern is by far the most haunted area of the old structure. If all the stories are to be believed, there are powerful forces at work in the sublevel tavern, which is called Planter's Tavern to commemorate James Habersham Jr.'s title of 'planter', meaning an agricultural producer and plantation owner.

One believer is Gail Thurmond, the talented and versatile piano player who entertains diners in Planters Tavern. But Gail is not just blessed with musical talent; she is one of the few people whom are gifted with special 'sight', the ability to see the spirit world. She claims to see a small African-American child in the tavern from time to time, or feel his presence. She even claims to have asked this small boy his name, and he replied 'Magumbo.'

Erika's Bottle Problem

Others have felt a presence downstairs, be it Magumbo or some other spirit. One waitress says she hears dice being thrown against the wall on a frequent basis in the hallway leading to the bathrooms. But by far the strangest story was told by Erika Williams, longtime bartender in the tavern. On occasion, according to Erika, the wine bottles will pop out of their cubbyhole in the wine rack by themselves. She has even been hit by a flying bottle or two in her time behind the bar—and event seen by eyewitnesses. The spirits have been known to flow pretty freely at the bar, but this would be considered taking that turn of phrase too literally when bartenders are being smacked by them. So in this case, Erika's supernatural experience was caused by being hit *by* the bottle, instead of the other way around.

Erika also related hearing the dice being thrown against the wall on several occasions, and claims that when she is in the vault, she will sometimes hear her name called when she knows she is all alone. But she smiled broadly when revealing one of the stranger places for a haunting: the ladies room. Apparently some women find their trip to the rest room anything but restful when they are mysteriously locked inside. The door was holding fast on its own, prompting the management to shave the edge of the door down, thinking that might alleviate the problem. But the dilemma of ladies being locked in the 'loo continued, so the staff even went to the extreme measure of removing the lock on the door. This drastic step has still not fixed the predicament—the door sans lock will still inexplicably lock itself for short periods.

A Savannah man who was well-known to the staff went down to the downstairs tavern one evening for a beverage. He had just gotten his drink when he saw a man at the other end of the bar in full Colonial dress. Thinking that the restaurant had hired someone in costume, he smiled and raised his glass. The Colonial gentleman did the same, sharing a toast. The waiter turned to the bartender and mentioned what an authentic- looking outfit the gentleman had on, and the bartender asked him what he was talking about. When he turned and motioned towards the man, there was no one to be seen.

So on this occasion in the tavern, a local shared a toast—with a ghost. This is thought to be the spirit of James Habersham, Jr., who had a reputation for being a fine and cordial host. The staff feels that he will check in from time to time, just to make sure that his former home is still being hospitable.

One night in the tavern, most of the staff had left, all but the bartender and the manager. The manager said to the bartender, "The upstairs is all clear." It was then that they could hear the sound of a woman sobbing, clearly emanating from the upstairs. The bartender turned to the manager and said, "Do you hear that?" The manager said, "No, I don't hear a thing, and neither do you. We're getting out of here!" They closed and left early, leaving dishes on tables, money in the register, and the safe unlocked.

In another instance, the sound of heavy coins being counted was heard coming from near the north fireplace in the tavern. A likely explanation is that gold was stored in this area at one time—a British transport ship named the HMS Expervier was transporting gold when it was captured by the Peacock, a U.S. warship, during the War of 1812.

And what of the Habershams, the family separated by an ocean of divided loyalty? Only in death did they resolve their bitter family conflict: they are buried together in Colonial Park Cemetery, father with sons, sons with father.

Some Erroneous Folklore

One story told about the Pink House which has no historical merit is that James Habersham hanged himself in the basement which is now the tavern. The erroneous story is that he learned of his wife's affair with the architect of the building and committed suicide.

The truth is less theatrical, yet much more uplifting. Habersham was a Revolutionary War hero, successful businessman, loving husband, and beloved father. It is the story of American triumph over adversity. Habersham died in 1799, and the cause of death is listed as 'declining health'. Burial of someone who had committed suicide was not permitted in consecrated ground, so the fact that James Habersham is buried with his father and brothers in Colonial Park Cemetery is yet another indicator that the story of Jr.'s hanging is false.

The Olde Pink House, 23 Abercorn St., is open nightly for dinner from 5:00 p.m. to 10:30 p.m. and for lunch Tuesday-Saturday at 11:00 a.m.

River Street Inn

Sitting on the bluff overlooking River Street is the River Street Inn. Portions of the Inn were built as early as 1817— the ground floor of the structure is constructed of ballast stones, which were brought as ballast in ships from Europe. This type of construction is common on the lower level of River Street. The upper three floors were added in 1853. The building used to be a place where cotton was stored and graded, but now it has been renovated into a beautiful inn.

The River Street Inn has another reputation, in addition to being some of the finest lodging in the city: a haven for haunted happenings.

Housekeepers claim to dislike the third floor of the Inn because of the westernmost hallway. Strange occurrences include unexplained footsteps that sound as if they are walking on hardwood, even though the hall is carpeted. The staff has even heard disembodied voices. The most disturbing part is that the housekeepers hear their *own* names being called. Doors have been known to open and slam mysteriously, which is something even experienced by this author.

A 'Slam' to the Psyche

I had heard many stories involving the Inn from the staff, and decided to check out the hallway in the Spring of 2003. I went down to the third floor and slowly began walking down the hallway in question. I am by no means a 'Ghostbuster' or a scientist, but I want to experience the areas about which I write—and there is a basic human curiosity in which one wonders what will happen to them in a haunted area. On several occasions I have been in the presence of what I would deem genuine paranormal phenomena, and in more than a couple of these I have felt a strange polarizing energy in the air. The only comparison I can offer (besides being ground zero in the event of a lightning strike, which is an event you never forget if it happens to you) is feeling static electricity, as if someone pulled a wool blanket out of the dryer and wrapped you in it. This is the feeling I experienced while walking down the hallway of the River Street Inn. Every nerve ending seemed to tingle as I walked.

Suddenly, about three quarters down the hallway, a door slammed hard behind me! I nearly jumped out of my skin. As I stood there with my heart pounding, I began to feel a little foolish. I had, in my own opinion, psyched myself up that I had psyched myself out, so to speak. I had perhaps so badly wanted an encounter with something unexplainable that I allowed myself to be frightened by what I assumed was a guest opening and then immediately slamming their door. The strange 'energized' sensation was gone, as well, and I began to feel that I perhaps imagined it.

I walked back up to the lobby and explained to the girl behind the front desk what had happened to me in the third floor hallway, poking fun at myself for being a little silly for being so scared by a door slamming. But she got an odd look, and asked for me to repeat myself. I told her again: "I went down to the third floor hallway and was scared silly by a slamming door. I swear Elizabeth, if that guest had slammed their door just a little harder, you'd have to call housekeeping to clean up the puddle I'd have left in the hall."

Elizabeth smiled as she tapped on her computer screen, and replied, "But there *aren't* any guests on the third floor right now. It's between check-out and check-in—the entire side on the third floor is completely empty right now." I protested, "Surely there must be a housekeeper up there?" She shook her head emphatically, and asked if I had seen a housekeeping cart in the hallway. I hadn't. "Maintenance?" I tried gamely. She again said no. I had been frightened by a door slamming in a hallway which was deserted except for me—at least by the living.

Several guests and staff have had encounters with an apparition in this same third floor hallway. The spectre appears to be male according to eyewitness accounts, dressed in clothes of a well-to-do 19th century businessman. In more than one instance the staff behind the front desk has been asked if there is a reenactment event in town. One young girl referred to him as 'the Monopoly Man', making a reference to the popular board game's instantly recognizable icon.

One desk clerk named Stan claims to have had a strange encounter late one evening. He was sitting behind the front desk, when out of the corner of his eye he saw a woman dressed in white enter the lobby. Busy at his desk, he gave her a quick glance and continued with his paperwork. She approached the desk, but turned and walked briskly away— and disappeared by walking straight through a solid brick wall. "I saw it with my own two eyes," he said.

Yet another staff member claims having an encounter with something she considers paranormal. "I was working all alone on the second floor near the bar," the young bartender said, "and I heard someone speaking in muffled tones. I walked out to see who it was, since the bar area was closed and was supposed to be deserted. There was no one there, so I went back to the bar and continued closing up, and then I heard the strange sound again—like a muffled cry, or someone choking back sobs. All the hair on the back of my neck stood up. When I peered down the hallway again, I saw a shadowy form enter the hallway, and walk right straight through a door without opening it." She added, "It's the only time I've ever seen or heard anything out of the ordinary, but once is enough for me!"

Amanda St. Vincent, who worked behind the front desk, claims to have had problems with the locking security mechanism on the front doors to the Inn that defy explanation. The lock is one that, when flipped at night, requires a room key for access. Amanda was having problems on a busy Saturday afternoon, because the switch controlling the mechanism kept flipping to the 'on' position, which had the unfortunate side-effect of locking out people who were attempting to check in. Amanda, who is a believer in the supernatural, spoke in a firm voice, asking the spirit to stop—doing so in front of paying customers at check-in. There were looks of astonishment when the problem immediately rectified itself. Apparently the ghosts at the Inn are well-trained.

M elonie's Antiques

Two things abound in the former warehouses that now comprise the restaurants, tourist shops, and bars of River Street: history, and hauntings. The construction of these buildings was primarily done in two stages. The bottom floors of most of River Street were built out of ballast stone around 1820, but the upper floors were not added until there was a need for office space in the 1850's and '60's. The backsides of these warehouses, facing Bay Street away from the river, have a series of bridges running above the back lane separating the buildings and Bay St. These bridges were where bidders on cotton, commonly called 'factors', would observe the cotton and grade it, and thus it became known as Factor's Walk.

Near the Abercorn ramp down to River Street, directly across from the River Street Inn, there sits a row of these former cotton warehouses, built in 1860. The lower floors were built in 1823 for Archibald Smith, a cotton merchant. Linked to Bay St. by Factor's Walk, the structure now houses Melonie's Antiques, one of the finer places in which to acquire items with a sense of history. Perhaps the spirits also like to visit their former possessions, or maybe they are just more comfortable surrounded by items that feel familiar, because Melonie's has a definite reputation for being haunted. Several apparitions have been seen, and the antique shop seems to also have a mischievous poltergeist with a penchant for the ultimate sin in the antiques business: it likes to break the merchandise.

✎Elizabeth & the Woman in Blue✎

Elizabeth, a worker at Melonie's, claims that before she worked at the antique store, she did not believe in ghosts, but has had so many experiences that the store has made her a believer. The owner, Melonie, had told her on many occasions that the store was haunted, but Elizabeth took the stories with a grain of salt. But on one afternoon a few years ago, Elizabeth had her first brush with the supernatural.

She was taking a quick break to feed change into the parking meter at which she had parked, leaving Melonie alone for a moment. Upon returning, she saw a woman in a blue pantsuit walk in ahead of her. She walked in and stepped behind the counter and waited, but could not see the woman anywhere. She stood at the counter for several quiet minutes before she started to get an inkling that she and Melonie were alone. She asked Melonie if she had seen anyone walk in ahead of her, and Melonie said she had—and described the woman perfectly, with a broad smile on her face. Elizabeth, not yet in on the joke, made a quick search of the store to see if she could be of any assistance, but she found nothing but empty aisles. The only way the woman in blue could have exited the store was to walk past the counter where Elizabeth had been waiting, but she knew the woman hadn't left. Melonie was still smiling when Elizabeth came back to the counter, because she had encountered the woman several times before, and the woman always entered the store, and then vanished into thin air.

Melonie has had her own odd occurrences. She has on many occasions heard strange footsteps coming from an area where a staircase was once located, but had been sealed up in a long-ago renovation. The lower portion of the stairs were removed to separate the antique store from the restaurant below, meaning that Melonie was hearing the tread of footsteps on stairs that no longer existed.

She has also seen doorknobs twist on their own on numerous occasions, and when she investigated, she found nothing but an empty room on the other side. "After hours one night I was working near the rest room, and saw the doorknob jiggle. I went over and pulled the door open, you know, thinking that someone was in there who didn't realize the store was closed. But the bathroom was completely empty."

Melonie claims that from time to time when the shop is quiet, she will hear something smash. Often times the item found broken will have flung itself several yards from the shelf on which it was placed, or will be found after she places the item with care far from the edge of the shelf—and the item will seemingly fling itself off the edge as soon as her back is turned.

It is the belief of this author that there are at least two, and possibly more, different entities in Melonie's Antiques. The 'Woman in Blue' is a classic apparition: someone who vanishes seemingly into thin air. But there is also a poltergeist, the mischievous and destructive presence who likes to break display items. Perhaps coincidence, but perhaps not, is the fact that during the interview for this story in December of 2003, the author had a strange experience with no easy explanation. Melonie was speaking about the strange instances of breaking knickknacks, and the author suddenly felt his glasses literally pushed partly off of his face, and one lens came inexplicably out of the wire frame, even though they had been recently tightened. The screw which held the lens in place was nowhere to be found, at least initially.

Melonie smiled knowingly, and simply said, "Things like that happen around here all the time." The missing screw was later found in the author's shirt pocket—which had been buttoned securely when the screw fell out.

B. Matthews Eatery

At the corner of East Bay and Habersham streets, a quiet, unassuming structure has ties to several chapters of Savannah's history. Now the home of B. Matthews Eatery, the building has a technical claim as one of the oldest buildings in Georgia. The lunch special of the house is the black-eyed pea cake sandwich, but a favorite of this author is the turkey, cheddar and apple sandwich on wheat berry bread.

I am told a lot of ghost stories. Often times these stories are nothing more than anecdotes, but there are those occasions where a ghost tale which I at first assume will be a little story grows into something much, much bigger: B. Matthews Eatery is a perfect example of this. The owner simply mentioned one day in passing that the restaurant was haunted, and I believed it would be a small story when I sat down to interview him. But he actually gave me two hours of his time, answering all of my (admittedly technical) historical questions in great detail.

One of my first questions was regarding the building's past. With the building's date listed in tax records as 1790, the owner explained that the documentation on the building was from its sale in 1791. No one, not even the Georgia Historical Society's records, has any definitive proof of the build date. The building is thought to have been cobbled together out of both a former building on the site as well as a sailing vessel that foundered in the harbor. Many of the old planks and beams which were used in the construction came from this seagoing vessel, including the large central beam in the center of the restaurant, which was the original ship's mast. Recognized as one of the oldest public taverns still to exist in America today, the current home of the bakery also has one of the oldest bar tops in the United States. The building could represent Savannah's history as a metaphor—both now serving a different purpose, and even a little cobbled together, but still beautiful.

⌾Savannah and her Seaport⌾

The structure has seen an era of amazing change in this Southern port city. By the early 1790's, the institution of slavery was in decline. The South was producing tobacco, rice, and a special strain of cotton (Sea Island cotton) that could be grown only in very sandy soil along the coast. Tobacco depleted the soil within very few years, and land was so cheap that tobacco planters never bothered to reclaim the soil by crop rotation— they simply moved farther west. The other crops— rice, indigo, corn, and a little wheat– would sustain a living but little else. Slaves were very expensive, not only to buy but to maintain; some Southern planters were beginning to believe that the institution of slavery was beginning to die out, since a slave's labor would sometimes not even pay for his or her upkeep.

But an invention changed the South forever. Inventor Eli Whitney, visiting nearby Mulberry Grove Plantation, had an intuitive grasp of machinery. He set to work on a device to make cleaning seeds out of cotton a simpler task. He succeeded beyond anyone's wildest dreams: his machine could do what used to be a day's worth of work for several men in less than an hour. He and his partner, Phineas Miller, tried to patent their invention in 1793, calling it a cotton gin. But the design proved so easy to copy, and copyright enforcement became impossible. They did not make the riches such a device should have rightfully provided. Embittered by his lack of profits, Whitney later went on to develop a system of interchangeable parts for firearms, a method of industrialization that very quickly spawned a new era of mass- production.

Eli Whitney was a benevolent man, but his concepts changed the face of the 19th century: here was a man who cared little for slavery, but his invention of the cotton gin encouraged a cruel system that endured for over 70 years. He also invented interchangeable parts, for which factories would be needed, as well as unskilled labor. Indeed, the problem lay not in just the brutal implementation of these differing methods of production, but Whitney's inventions requiring plantations and factories would be at the ideological root of one of the greatest crises the United States has ever faced.

Savannah changed greatly because of King Cotton. Her economy grew exponentially—in 1790, cotton exports were 1,000 bales. By 1819, *90,000* bales were exported. What had previously been a squalid little town was now a bustling seaport. Banks opened just to handle the sudden influx of cash. A society based primarily on bartering had to readjust to having money to spend. And of course, slaves were in high demand. Many made fortunes by the sweat and blood of those bound in chains.

Ties to Slavery

The building now housing B. Matthews Bakery & Eatery saw every bit of that change in Savannah's destiny. My interview with the owner unveiled quite a bit of the old tavern's history. One of his conditions in agreeing to be interviewed for this volume was that the history must be told the right way. "I heard a tour guide saying that George Washington visited here in his tour of Savannah in 1791, and had a cup of coffee here. With the types that this place would draw during that period, I really doubt Washington would be popping in for a visit!" Indeed, he has his history very much in order: the bar was a haven for smugglers, privateers, and lovers of strong spirits. There is an underground tunnel leading from the river to the basement of the old structure, providing extensive evidence that the sublevel area was used as a storage area for imported slaves. All throughout the lower level there are large iron rings attached to the wall and the stairs where these pitiful souls were once chained.

The importation of slaves was banned by the Georgia legislature in 1798, preceding federal laws by ten years. But unofficially and illicitly, of course, the practice continued. The renegade slave ships were brutal places, as evidenced by Maya Angelou's fire-and-brimstone words inscribed on the monument on River Street commemorating these unfortunate victims of slavers. These slaves would be moved from the river back up through the tunnels, which hid them from the eyes of the authorities. Another reason the underground passages were used was because the slaves being transported were in such awful condition, often being covered in blood or excrement, that the slavers shielded them from public view not from any fear of prosecution, but from fear of their value being hurt by perception of 'damaged goods'. The tunnel may also have been used by smugglers, or perhaps by those privateer crews in need of some able-bodied crewmen, and willing to secure their 'fresh meat' through kidnapping.

It was already into its second century as a tavern when it was bought by a Greek man with the last name Mataxas in 1910. The family still owns the structure. He served as a deckhand on a sailing vessel and jumped ship in Boston in 1907, and by 1910 he had made his way to Savannah. He met and married a local girl, and they had four children. Mataxas bought the bar, and continued to run the place as a tavern in spite of Prohibition.

The owner recounts what one of Mataxas' sons told him: that he has fond memories of watching his father flavor the illegal gin. The tavern was a 'Speakeasy' throughout the '20's, often hosting parties where the illicit beverages flowed freely. After Prohibition ended, one of the doors became another means of selling alcohol: the old tavern had sidewalk service, selling bottles to passersby.

The bar also had an interesting solution to Segregation: the two rooms were joined by the bar on the southern side, which had a passage between for the bartenders—one white, the other black, each serving their respective clientele. The clientele was not allowed to mix, but the bartenders worked side-by-side, a strange instance of the 1950's idea of 'Separate but Equal'. The arrangement turned bloody, however. According to the owner, the black bartender began dating the daughter of his counterpart, and the enraged wife of the white bartender shot and killed her daughter's boyfriend in a dispute over their illicit affair.

৵Adventures in Renovating৵

The old bar was renovated several times over the years, including several times where the result was less than satisfactory. I was shown a picture of the condition of the place when the most recent renovations began: the entire place had been painted midnight blue with yellow piping. "They painted over the three pink marble balustrades on the bars," the owner said, disgust creeping into his voice. "Painted it— that's pink marble from the only pink marble mine in the state, in

Tate, Georgia." And it was during the last renovations that the owner realized that the building came with more than an ugly paint job: the place was haunted.

Things would turn up missing or moved to a new location while the work was going on, mostly their tools. While this is not unusual on a job site, they related some humorous instances where the screwdrivers would disappear for hours, only to be found in plain view. Drill bits would vanish. The toolbox mysteriously disappeared for a time, and then was found nearby, apparently tossed against the wall.

In another incident right as the restaurant was opening, the portion scale, which is vital to the operation of a bakery, went missing. The staff hunted high and low for the scale, but it was nowhere to be found. The owner finally threw up his hands three days later and went and bought another scale—an expense as a new businessman he could ill afford. When he returned and was installing the new scale, he noticed the old scale in plain view on one of the tables. "There is no way we could have missed seeing the scale there in the center of the table. It was pretty obvious at that point we were dealing with a ghost who liked to hide things and then give them back."

There were other happenings: "I was working late one night, trying to get the place open. I was cleaning the floors on my hands and knees, and suddenly, I felt someone in the room with me. I didn't know what to do, so I started talking. I introduced myself, and explained what I was trying to do; I said I hoped that it was okay, and that we could exist peacefully in the old place together. I apologized if I was intruding but we had to open the restaurant soon. I also added that if the presence could, or felt like it, could it help me?

"The presence stayed for a while, and then finally I felt 'them' leave."

Playful Ghost

Perhaps the appeal worked. In spite of the playful disappearances of tools and other spectral mayhem, the restaurant known as B. Matthews opened on schedule. But it was not without a few hitches: one of the owners was presented with a special knife set that cost $1200 to celebrate the opening. Shortly after the knives were given, two of them disappeared. "We hunted high and low for them, and I was beginning to suspect that they had been stolen. Finally we found the knives—they hadn't been misplaced *or* stolen. They had been stuck in the wooden floor."

Salt and pepper shakers have been thrown across the restaurant with such force they hit the wall. "Good thing they're plastic," he joked. Also being thrown from time to time was a drawer face behind the register. "It wasn't attached to a drawer," he explained, "Perhaps at one time it was, but at this point it was just decorative, so we wedged it in place." The problem was, it wouldn't stay put. The drawer face would pop out constantly, and with a surprising degree of violence. "Numerous times, it has hit the back of the register stand," the owner explained, and showed me the spot where it happened. The space between the drawer face and the register was roughly three feet, and it would take more than a draft from the basement or the groan of a shifting building to pop the drawer that distance. "I never get the impression that the presence is unfriendly, or wants to harm anyone. I think they just want to be noticed," he says. "We finally wound up just leaving that drawer face out—it's a little unsightly, but if it makes the ghost happy, I'll leave it." In another case of spectral disobedience, the spirit has also been known to open the cabinet doors behind the work space at random times, apparently taking pleasure from the fact that the staff will run into them, occasionally falling.

The owner reported that not all of the spirits at B. Matthews fall under this 'friendly yet mischievous' category. One friend of the owners named Scott popped in for a visit. Scott was described as very large in stature, but also with a sensitivity to all things spiritual and supernatural. Scott asked to see the basement. The owner took him down and was showing him around when Scott suddenly fell ill. "He said he felt two spirits down there that were very unhappy. He was trembling." Scott was so affected by his visit to the downstairs area that he had to cut his visit short and leave prematurely. It was only then that it occurred to the owner that the area had once housed slaves, and that someone as sensitive as Scott would surely pick up on the residual feelings of those bound in chains.

Recently I appeared onscreen as a local expert on the paranormal for the PBS documentary "Haunted South," which was filmed on location at B. Matthews. The restaurant never fails to cooperate, and it wasn't necessary for re-enactors to stage historic events as enough ghosts showed up— as if on cue— to lend a hand, all of which was captured on camera.

Visitors to B. Matthews are encouraged to bring their cameras.

B. Matthews is located at the corner of East Bay and Habersham streets. Open every day for breakfast, lunch and dinner, from 8 a.m. until 10 p.m. Sunday brunch from 9 a.m. to 3 p.m.

R ene Rondolia

The story of Rene Rondolia Asch, the seven-foot giant who supposedly terrorized Savannah in the early days of the 1800's, is a bit of folklore that has become a Savannah tradition. Many different versions have been told throughout the years. Some have likened the story to a real-life Frankenstein's monster, elaborating on the central theme of a misunderstood killer. Others have compared him to Lenny, from Steinbeck's *Of Mice and Men.* However, the historical record supports absolutely none of the wild tales told about this murderer of women and children. Every historian asked about this particular ghost story had the same thing to say: "It never happened." One in particular asked that it not be included in this volume, and when pressed for a reason, she explained that the last name 'Asch' was the name of a prominent Jewish family and to tack their name on the end was disrespectful. For that reason that last name will be omitted for the remainder.

Some have credited the story of Rene Rondolia as being an influence on Mary Shelley's book *Frankenstein.* The story goes that Mary Shelley met Joseph Bevan, Savannah socialite and historian, through his friend and her father, William Godwin, and Bevan recounted the tale to Shelley. There is no historical evidence to support this theory, and in fact Bevan visited Godwin during a time when Shelley and Godwin were estranged, so a meeting between the author and Bevan is unlikely. Shelley, oddly enough, dedicated the book to her father, and it shows his influence. Shelley never mentioned a Savannah connection to the book, not even in her journal. Since no serious scholar has ever made a connection between a bit of Savannah folklore with Mary Shelley's work, one must, in the absence of other evidence, believe the experts: Shelley was influenced by her father, Milton's *Paradise Lost*, and Ovid's *Metamorphoses.*

This tale is exactly that, a tale, and it more than likely was concocted to frighten kids around campfires. Amongst Savannah folklore, this particular story is about as famous as the 'bloody hook on the car door'. It was more than likely used to frighten children and warn them against the dangers of staying out too late. It is only with that caveat that the story is recounted here:

On the eastern side of Savannah in the early 1800's, there was an area known as Foley's Alley. It was the blue-collar district, where the tradesmen (carpenters, shipbuilders, iron workers, brick masons, etc.) lived. As the story goes, the terror began there, because in September 1804 a doctor was summoned in the middle of the night to Foley's Alley. He was summoned to deliver a child. Now in those days, doctors did not deliver children; that was a job for midwives. But this woman, Maria, was in agony. She had been in labor for 3 days, and she began begging for the doctor.

According to legend, the doctor arrived, and had no idea what to do for this woman. He had to perform a very crude form of surgery on Maria that night. *He had to break that poor woman's pelvis* in order to deliver her child. A lot of whiskey was doubtlessly involved— both for her, and for the doctor. The reason he had to break her pelvis is because her child weighed in at *sixteen pounds*, four ounces. Rene Rondolia came into the world under strange circumstances that evening.

Rene was a big baby. He grew into an even bigger boy. At the age of 15, he stood at over seven feet tall, and weighed over three hundred pounds. He was very simple of mind. He spoke no English, only broken archaic French. He learned this from his mother, who was descendant from a French Huguenot. Rene roamed the back lanes and streets of Foley's Alley at night. He was simple of mind and didn't know right from wrong. He would catch animals— anything he could get his hands on— cats, small dogs, squirrels, and play with them for a while. Because he didn't know his own strength, he would break their necks.

The people of Foley's Alley tolerated Rene Rondolia. But this changed when the body of a young child was found on Warren Square, the western edge of Foley's Alley. Her neck was broken. General consensus was that Rene had caught this young girl and murdered her. The people of Foley's Alley, already angry over the great fire that had devastated our city in 1820, dragged him to the center of Warren Square. There they hanged him from a live oak on the southwest corner of Warren Square. The tree that they supposedly used still stands today. It took several men to haul Rene off of the ground, and it took a long time for Rene to strangle on the rope. His neck did not break.

Imagine the shock and horror of those people responsible for the execution of Rene *when those child killings continued into 1821.* Was it Rene? Could he have come back from the grave and continued to kill? Or did they put an innocent person to death?

Many people, including several prominent Savannah citizens, have reported seeing someone walking out at night in Foley's Alley. This person is reported to be over seven feet tall, and when he reaches Warren Square, he will look to the tree on the southwest corner of the square and then fade from sight. Others have reported seeing just a hulking shadow moving across the grass.

Credit this tale with inspiring more sleepless nights on camping trips than any other story in Savannah.

Willink House~ 426 E. St. Julian Street

The small 1845 house located on the northwest corner of Price and St. Julian Streets has both a storied history and a haunted past. The house itself is also well-traveled. It was originally built for Henry F. Willink and stood just south of Oglethorpe Avenue at the corner of Price and Perry Streets, but was moved later to the present location. The structure is indicative of a type of building that was popular from the late 18th to mid 19th century in Savannah: small, simple, and mobile if need be.

Willink was a shipbuilder, and lived in the house for roughly ten years. He is an important figure in Savannah because he served as one of the chief contractors in Savannah whose services provided ships for the fledgling Confederate Navy. When the C.S. Navy was formed, the Secessionists had not one single ship. But Willink helped change all that, and quickly helped build the Confederates a fighting force with his shipyards. He built two of the three ironclad vessels produced in Savannah. Unfortunately, the technology of building ironclad warships was so new, that while the armored ships were impressive to view, the seaworthiness and effectiveness were less than satisfactory.

The first ironclad produced in the Willink shipyard, the *C.S.S. Georgia*, was so heavily armored and underpowered that she could scarcely move. She had to be towed into position, and was much more effective as a floating battery than a fighting ship. But Willink should not shoulder the blame for the vessel's shortcomings; this was an experimental technology, and was called "The Ladies Gunboat", not because of any perceived shortcomings to the craft, but because she was paid for by $115,000 raised by the Ladies' Gunboat Association. The problems with Willink's vessels were common amongst the new ironclads, be they produced by North or South.

The second (and last) ironclad produced by Willink's shipyards was a monster called the *C.S.S. Savannah*. While fearsome in her armament, she was also brutal on her crew. One sailor wrote of the conditions aboard another ironclad, which is indicative of the experiences of all Confederate sailors forced to live aboard such ships: "There is no ventilation at all. I would defy anyone in the world to tell when it is day or when night if he is confined below without any way of marking time... I would venture to say that if a person were blindfolded and carried below and turned loose he would imagine himself in a swamp, for the water is trickling in all the time and everything is so damp." This would be a sign of the conditions of the seagoing iron monsters produced by Willink, as well. The *Savannah* was destroyed by Rebel seamen to avoid her capture by Union forces in late 1864.

The occupying Union forces charged Willink with aiding the enemy. Mr. Willink freely admitted that charge, which so impressed the authorities that they let him go.

Tragedy in the Shipyards

But while Willink had a successful career making ships for the Confederate Navy, one area of his life still pained him: his wife's death in a visit to the shipyards, years before. She visited him aboard ship, and in a senseless accident she took a misstep and plunged into the swift Savannah current. Unable to swim, she drowned.

Henry was devastated. He absorbed himself in his work, often times pacing the floor of his little cottage. He sometimes left for work at odd hours, slamming the door to his house and trudging down to the river to work out his frustrations in the middle of the night.

It has been previously reported that the small cottage would sometimes be the scene of this nocturnal ritual of Mr. Willink's: from time to time the phantom sound of the door slamming shut has been heard, by neighbors and passerby, when no one can be seen leaving the dwelling. This occurred before the house was moved to its present location in 1964—perhaps the change in scenery has calmed the nervous energy, or perhaps Mr. Willink has finally found the peace that eluded him, so many years before. Or is it possible that the two lovers are rejoined?

A Place of Learning

But it is from the time period after Willink owned the house that some residual energy still lingers. In the years before the Emancipation Proclamation, it was considered illegal to teach slaves to read or write. It has been said that the house became an illicit school for African-American children in the years spanning from 1855 to just before the outbreak of the Civil War. A white female teacher began teaching the slaves to read and basic math skills, even though this was prohibited by law at the time. She taught the slave children to calculate by using sweets, which if added properly became that child's reward for solving the problem correctly.

She was eventually found out, and was given an option by the authorities: she could face arrest and a fine, or she could leave town. Either way, her school was gone forever. The teacher reluctantly agreed to leave the city, and she bade farewell to her students and departed Savannah, never to return. This sad chapter of American history faded into the past.

Or did it? Subsequent owners have reported finding sweets moved from their kitchen into other areas of the house such as the living room. Those same bits of candy have been found arranged into what appear to be rows of simple mathematical problems. Could the essence of these children be revisiting the house they knew as a school so many years before? Could they be engaging in that familiar activity, perhaps hoping to receive those same remembered rewards?

This house has known tragedy in the form of Henry Willink's ill-fated wife, but the greater tragedy is those children, denied a proper education because of ignorance and racism. Maybe those young ones make an appearance from time to time to let us know that they have not forgotten their lessons, or their teacher's kindness. It seems the education they received taught them math and writing skills, but the lesson they have taken to heart was their teacher's compassion.

Savannah Harley-Davidson

The shops along River Street sometimes have stories that are difficult to explain. It seems that several ghosts have taken up residence at the Harley-Davidson shop on the eastern side of River Street. Like so many current shops along the river, this formerly was a cotton warehouse.

Members of the staff have reported strange sounds, primarily from the second floor, which is supposedly where slaves were once housed, as well as being a humidor when the shop was a cigar store.

Then other bizarre occurrences started to take place. According to a Savannah Morning News article which ran October 31st, 2000, Sue Barnes, who worked at the store, saw a man in a suit and tie out of the corner of her eye during a moment she knew herself to be alone. "I thought maybe we had a ghost," she said. According to the article, the faucet in the upper level bathroom was known to turn on, and the toilet had been known to mysteriously flush. But the truly mysterious occurrences were yet to come, and took place much more recently than the year 2000.

Former staff member Laura O'Neil arrived early one Sunday morning, and found the children's rack of clothes on the second floor in disarray. She straightened them and began getting the store ready to open. When she happened to pass by the clothes once again, she noticed that once again were hanging askew, so she approached them. It was then that she felt a strange cold feeling, a feeling like an icy gust of wind, and Laura heard a child laughing. "I decided those clothes could stay where they were," deadpanned Laura.

Former staff member Melissa Pashea has had numerous experiences with the spirit, whom she has named 'Boo'. She was working in the upstairs when she began to smell cigar smoke. She called down to the first floor to another staff member, who also smelled the cigar. She even called out to see if someone was on the second level with her, and got no response, which is when she decided to confront the spirit directly. She said, "Boo, don't be smoking up here." The cigar smell vanished instantly.

Melissa also said that she has found footprints in the dust on one of the tables upstairs. The marks in the dust were of small bare feet, all over the case.

Merchandise is often found moved when the staff opens up for the morning, primarily on the second floor. A strange cold spot has also been experienced by many of the staff, and also by this author, on the second level that defies explanation. The temperature seems to drop suddenly by what feels like twenty degrees. The only comparison to the feeling when stepping into that cold spot is when an elevator dips unexpectedly before the doors open.

Is the children's laugh heard by a staff member the presence haunting the Savannah Harley-Davidson? Or is it the man wearing the suit and tie? Perhaps time will tell, but one thing is certain: staff members are on their toes when they venture upstairs, because those ghosts have proven to be 'hog' wild.

Hampton Lillibridge House

The Hampton Lillibridge House is a beautiful light blue three-story structure tucked away close to the river in one of the oldest parts of the Historic District, but its beautiful exterior belies the strange and even malevolent spirits within. It has what is referred to as a 'widow's walk' along the roof, and the roof itself is a gambrel-style more commonly found in the seacoast towns of New England. This wonderful example of 18th century architecture was built in 1799 by Hampton Lillibridge, and was originally constructed about three blocks away from its present location on St. Julian Street. Over the years it has been the private residence of the Lillibridge family, a boarding house, and spent the 20th century as a tenement before being bought by Jim Williams, he of *Midnight in the Garden of Good and Evil* fame, who moved it in 1963 to the present location.

⁞ "We're Leaving!" ⁞

It was during Williams' restoration that events turned tragic: when the house was being prepared for the move to the current location, the house next door collapsed and a worker was killed.

Once the house was moved, the brick masons began to complain that they could hear the sounds of people walking around or even running on the upper floors of the house. This was impossible, since the upper floors didn't even have stairs. Jim Williams lived across the street at the time, and he was confronted by a group of these workers one night. They had been frightened by the strange noises coming from the house, and they explained to him, "Mr. Williams, there are some people in your house over yonder and those people do not work for you! We're leaving." Williams himself described that the sounds were not simply the noises of an old house settling—instead sounding like doors being slammed, furniture broken, and unseen people were laughing, stomping and yelling.

One night when Williams was out of town, the masons once again threw down their tools and refused to work because of all the strange noises. Three of Williams' friends were out on the street when this occurred, and one of the friends who was a non-believer went inside to prove that the masons were simply being ridiculous. The other friends outside heard a scream come from the house which seemed to come from the top floor, so they ran inside. There they found their friend on the top floor, lying on his back near an open chimney shaft. He claimed that an unseen force had surrounded him on the top floor, feeling like he had walked into a pool of cold water, and he found himself walking very much against his will towards the hole for the shaft in the floor. The only way he could escape this urge to pitch himself headfirst down the shaft was to fall instead to the floor.

While the three of them knelt there in the floor, one of the men said, "The only thing I know that Jim Williams could do is to have the house exorcised," and at that moment the men heard a woman's scream—and the scream came from *in between them*! One of them jumped to his feet and asked, "What on earth was that?!" and the scream was heard once again. The three men ran for their lives. Once out on the street, they saw the figure of a man standing at the top middle window wearing a white suit and a silk cravat. He glared at them for a moment, and then he vanished.

Amazingly, Williams wasn't told this story until *after* he had moved into the Lillibridge House some weeks later. He complained to friends that he was often awakened by the sound of footsteps in an empty house, and once had a dark figure appear in the doorway, which then approached his bed. Williams was about to cry out in terror, when suddenly the figure vanished a few feet from him.

Protection From Ghosts?

Williams took steps to protect himself: he began keeping a loaded Luger pistol within easy reach on his bedside table, presumably to *shoot* the ghost if it ever came back. He also brought in an Episcopalian Bishop to perform the rite of exorcism.

This Bishop performed both a blessing ceremony and an exorcism on the house, but it apparently didn't work. Within ten days, the phenomena were back. In one instance, Williams was awakened by strange noises. He then chased his spectral intruder from room to room until finally a door slammed directly in his path, which then locked itself, ending the chase.

One night, Williams was at an auction. He came home to find the maid standing in the carport, afraid to go back inside despite the fact that it was raining. She reported feeling a "masculine presence" that made her uneasy; she had also heard the sound of rattling, grinding chains coming from somewhere in the house. On many occasions, neighbors often reported the sight of strange lights in the windows, and the sounds of parties heard out on the street below. These were seen on nights that the house was empty, and Williams was out of town.

The subsequent owners have reported strange sounds, and have a hard time keeping maids or babysitters for any length of time. A downstairs door was found pried open—*from the inside*. One couple living in the house became so curious about the strange activity in the house that they called in a team from Duke University, who studied the house at length. It was the determination of the team from Duke that this was the most haunted house they have ever encountered.

The couple that currently lives in the house doesn't talk of ghosts. The reason is because they value their privacy. This is a popular spot for ghost tours, and they simply want to be left alone. A plaque on the side of the house announces 'Private Residence', a clear indication that the current residents find ghosts less disturbing than being interrupted by curiosity seekers.

Underneath the front porch, there is a light shade of blue. This is called 'Haint Blue' by the Geechee people, which are our superstitious Island culture in the area, a culture that is even today involved in voodoo and the occult. This term 'haint' translates into 'ghost'. This color symbolizes water, which in the same superstitions an evil spirit will not cross. Outside of the supernatural benefit to this color, there is a practical one, as well. Any shade of sky blue underneath a front porch overhang will keep wasps away. Wasps are incredibly gullible creatures, and they believe that anything sky blue in color is the sky.

Around the property there is a brick wall, and lining the wall is a row of broken glass. This is something done since Colonial days to discourage intruders, and it has the added benefit of being a little more attractive than barbed wire. But a close look at the wall will reveal something surprising: one corner of the wall is directly touching another house adjacent to the property. Why would broken glass be needed to keep intruders from jumping a wall that they would have no way of crossing? It makes no sense until you consider that another belief of that superstitious Island culture is that a row of broken glass will keep *all* intruders away—earthly or otherwise. Broken glass lining walls is something you'll find in Cuba, New Orleans, and up and down the Lowcountry area.

507 E. St. Julian St. is a private residence. The owners do not open their house to tours. Please respect their privacy.

The Pirates' House

Thus after Dangers past, now safe and well

The Story to our Friends we often tell,

And they to Recompense us for our Tale

Do Strive to Drown us in a Cup of Ale.

"The Third Journal of Jeremy Roch" (1699)

Very close to the Savannah River on East Broad Street, one of the oldest structures in Savannah sits in an area called Old Fort. Some claim the structure was constructed as early as 1753, but others place it at a more conservative 1794. It is known today as the Pirates' House Restaurant. Little can be confirmed about the early days of the structure other than it was used as a sailor's tavern, but what is known is that members of the staff have said for years that areas of the Pirates' House are haunted.

Many stories have circulated about the Pirates' House—it is said to be where Robert Louis Stevenson wrote a portion of *Treasure Island*, and that he used it as a setting for where the bloodthirsty pirate Captain Flint died while asking for rum. Many Savannahians claim that Captain Flint's ghost still haunts the rooms of the house. However, Flint was a fictional character in Stevenson's epic tale. Some also say that Edward Teach, also known as Blackbeard roamed the halls, and some claim he still does. This story is also easy to discount, since Edward Teach died in November of 1718, a full fifteen years before Savannah was even founded, and thirty-five years before the earliest possible completion of the Pirates' House.

The truth about the Pirates' House is much more complicated. Did pirates really raise tankards of ale at the bar? Or is it nothing more than a lot of stories and a marketing scheme?

✎History of Pirates in the Area∿

What we know is that the so-called 'Golden Age of Piracy' existed from 1680 till 1730. In the early part of the 18ᵗʰ century, the British Royal Navy finally got enough control over the Americas to finally start ridding the oceans in that area of pirates. Since Savannah was not established until 1733, it appears unlikely that the Pirates' House was a haven for bloodthirsty buccaneers, because it had suddenly become a very dangerous business to be in.

After an exhaustive search of available records, the only account linking Savannah and piracy was in the journal of Peter Gordon, who was one of the original colonists in 1733. His story, occurring before Savannah was even established, describes the colonists' ship the *Anne* running across a strange and suspicious-looking vessel. Gordon writes, "...We were alarmed by a sloop who as soon as he perceived us standing along shore, emediately (sic) changed his course and bore down upon us, which... made us conclude that he must... be a pirate..." Gordon related that the craft was flying colors which appeared Spanish, and the craft veered away soon after being fired upon. Gordon also noted that "the pilote (sic) whome we had on board said he hade some knowledge of him that he hade been a pirate, and that he certainly would have plundered us hade he not found we were too strong for him." In a humorous aside, Gordon also commended the women of the *Anne*, taking notice of their bravery in that they asked to be permitted to load the weapons and even to fight alongside the men, but "some of our men who hade been noted the whole voyage for noisy bullying fellows, were not to be found on this occassion but skulked either in the hold or between decks."

If this is the only recorded instance of a pirate being sighted near Savannah, the odds of 'bloodthirsty buccaneers' being in Savannah in 1753 are unlikely, but not impossible. Also clouding the issue was the fact that while piracy was very much against the law, a practice known as privateering was acceptable to the English government, as long as the privateers attacked French or Spanish shipping. Piracy was the outlaw practice of preying on merchant ships and raiding coastal towns for profit. It differed from privateering, which consisted of the same actions, because privateers were sanctioned by a government to be conducted against an enemy during wartime. These privateers were in many cases a lot worse than pirates, because pirates would often just relieve the ships of cargo, whereas privateers would steal the cargo, kill the crew, and sell the vessel. In fact, pirate ships were more democratic than most realize, because they actually elected captains and the loot was shared more or less equally amongst the crew. It was the privateer who more closely resembled the modern misconceived idea of the 'savage pirate on the high seas'.

Jean Lafitte, often called a pirate, was actually a privateer hired by the British government: he raided enemy shipping, and both he and the Crown reaped the rewards. Lafitte indeed did visit Savannah. Indeed, the newspapers of the time were full of accounts of problems with privateers trying to recruit crews from the local populace. In fact, there is a stone in Colonial Park Cemetery that exists as a testament to the brutality of privateers—Jacob R. Taylor was killed by a French privateer crew, and his friends listed that the French crew attacked and stabbed the unarmed Mr. Taylor as he strolled the streets of Savannah.

So the question of whether or not pirates really did inhabit the old bar on East Broad St. is not an easy one to answer. Technically, the answer is: probably not. However, since most people's concept of a savage pirate is actually closer to the true definition of a privateer, and since first English and later French privateers did sail Savannah's waters, then the answer in the spirit of the law is yes. But true piracy was seeking less-civilized waters at that time, such as the Indian and Pacific Oceans.

The Tunnel

One feature of the Pirates' House is the rumored secret passageway, long since sealed that ran from the basement of the House to the seaport. It was with this passageway that sea captains would arrange for sailors to be shanghaied, a practice also known by a more formalized title: impressment. It is said that many men fell prey to this barbaric practice, including one Savannah policeman walking the dreaded beat of 'Foley's Alley'. This same kidnapped policeman awoke aboard a strange vessel. He was forced to work as a privateer, and it took him two years to finally make his way back to Savannah. Again, it is doubtful that true pirates would feel the need for such an arrangement, because serving on a pirate crew was so profitable. No, it would be far more likely that a tyrannical privateer captain would engage in such practices of smuggling unconscious men to serve as crewmen; that, or an English Navy Captain.

Likely, many men who enjoyed a drink at the old seaman's bar on Broad Street wound up waking up aboard ship, heads pounding either from drugs or a wallop, bound for ports unknown. Whether the tunnel actually exists is immaterial—and Savannah is rife with secret tunnels—the reality is that even if the rumored passageway is just the stuff of legend, the practice of shanghaiing men and boys was quite common, and not just limited to Savannah. All seaport cities had a problem with impressment of crews.

The tunnel is said to begin in the brick cellar beneath what is known as the Captain's Room. And it is in this area at the cellar stairs that most of the staff feels that the supernatural happenings occur at the restaurant. Voices of men have been heard echoing out of this area at times it has been known to be empty.

The Staff's Accounts

The Travel Channel program 'America's Most Haunted Places-Savannah' featured the Pirates' House. One account was from a cook who saw an apparition one night, which from his description could be nothing but an 18th- or early 19th- century seafaring man. He was working alone in the kitchen, and the stranger walked through the area, pausing only to glare at him briefly. The sailor then walked *through* the door without opening it. The cook described him as looking incredibly threatening, and it was not coincidentally the last time the cook has worked alone in the kitchen. The cook also will not enter the kitchen without his large gold crucifix, which he wears as a talisman around his neck, which he believes protects him from further spectral visits.

A former server named Lisa recounted her story for this author one night. She had always been curious about the old tunnel under the restaurant, so one night she mustered her courage. Lisa initially tried to get a few friends to accompany her, but no one else was brave enough to go into the deserted space with her, so against her better judgment she went alone. She entered the passageway, and immediately felt a chill. As she progressed, she felt more and more ill and woozy. Waves of nausea struck her, and finally she had to abandon her trek down the passage. She retreated her way back up into the restaurant, but her sick feeling did not fully disappear until she left to go home. She initially thought that perhaps she had inhaled some fume or vapor that had made her dizzy and ill, but she felt it every night when she returned to work at the Pirate's House after that night she explored the tunnel. She began to believe that some sort of psychic energy given off by the spirits at the House perhaps was making her ill for invading the passageway. She finally quit two weeks later, and in a bit of irony began to work at the 17Hundred90 Inn and Restaurant, which has its own share of ghosts.

Fortunately for Lisa, the ghosts in 17Hundred90 have been more receptive to her presence, and several of her occurrences are recounted in that chapter. It is the opinion of this author that perhaps in her experience at the Pirate's House she was reliving the drugged and woozy state of many of the shanghaied men, in years now departed, which passed through the very tunnel in which she first had that feeling.

Hard-Hearted Hannah's

The staff on occasion has experienced bizarre smells not normally associated with a restaurant. These olfactory manifestations have been described as roses, copper or even the smell of blood. Strange lights and voices have also been known to emanate from the upper floors, which in years gone by were rooms for rent to sailors. There was for many years an upstairs jazz bar, Hard-Hearted Hannah's, in this portion of the restaurant. A former server, Brittney, recounted several stories involving bizarre happenings in Hannah's. She was once back in the prep room, cleaned out the coffeepots and pushed them onto one of the metal prep tables, far from the edge. She turned and walked out through the swinging door, and heard a loud crash behind her. She walked back into the prep room and found the coffeepots smashed on the floor—somehow they had hurled off of the table with enough force to crash against the far wall. There was no one in the back room, so the pots had apparently moved by themselves.

In a similar instance with another server, a girl whom Brittney had trained was closing by herself one night, and she called Brittney late at night begging her to come back down to the restaurant. The girl claimed that the coffeepots had jumped off of one of the back tables by themselves and smashed on the floor. The girl refused to close Hannah's by herself because of the incident. When I asked Brittney why coffeepots would shatter on a regular basis in the old structure, she smiled, and told me her theory. "Maybe there's a ghost of some old sailor who didn't like us drinking coffee. Maybe he wanted us to have rum, instead." This, of course, is just as good a supposition as any—and makes a great story: the ghost who doesn't like to drink alone.

Brittney also said that she would see people from time to time out of the corner of her eye—people that would then disappear. "I'd just catch a quick glimpse, like someone flitting by, and then they'd be gone," she said. She also related that there was a stairwell connecting the upper bar with the downstairs restaurant, and on several occasions she would feel a presence. "I'd suddenly have the feeling that I was not alone," she claimed firmly. Several of the staff would refuse to walk down the stairs alone, preferring instead to walk the more circuitous route of walking outside to get to the Pirates' House.

After changing hands twice, the new ownership of the Pirates' House restaurant completed an extensive renovation in 2009, which removed one-third of the sprawling complex known as the Hideaways, where paranormal activity was routinely reported. The Herb House, formerly the office and research laboratory of local expert Murray Silver, has been turned into dining rooms. Past visitors to the site will return to find the Tunnel experience to have been sanitized by renovation and no one of Silver's expertise to guide an exploration of the property.

Trustees Garden

On the far eastern side of Savannah, right next to the Pirates' House, sits Trustees Garden. Named for the group that financed James Edward Oglethorpe's founding of Savannah, the area has been recently renovated into a cultural center. Now no longer used for its original agricultural purpose, the area is part of the new but just as vital lifeblood of Georgia's First City: tourist dollars. Included in this plot of ground are some of the oldest buildings in Georgia—and some of the oldest stories. It is perhaps no coincidence that this area of the city was at one time predominantly Irish and African American; both cultures have a penchant for stories involving ghosts, apparitions, and messages from beyond.

Shortly after arriving in Savannah in 1733, Oglethorpe established the experimental Trustees' Garden, which was originally a 10-acre garden located on the east end of Bay Street. Botanists were sent from England to see which plants would flourish in Savannah. They attempted to grow mulberry trees for silk, grapes for wine and other crops. Most of the plants did not survive the harsh Georgia climate and the experiment was by and large a failure. From this garden, however, came the original peach trees and cotton which eventually became major crops in the South. By 1755, the area had been converted to commercial use.

The area does serve as setting for one of the most important events in American history. On August 10th, 1776, the Declaration of Independence was read in Savannah. It was first read to the Council at Reynolds Square, and again outside the council house to an excited crowd. It was then read in front of a Liberty Pole located either in Johnson Square or at Tondee's Tavern. The confusion as to the location of the third reading probably stems from the copious amounts of celebratory drink used to toast the finer points of the document. The last reading of the Declaration was near the residences comprising the Trustees Garden, where a holiday was declared. The day was further celebrated by cannon firings and a mock funeral procession for King George III, complete with coffin.

The historic area was in danger of being demolished by the Savannah Gas Company in the early 1940's, but a woman named Mary Hillyer issued a call to action to save the area from the wrecking ball. With the help of her husband and the board of directors at the gas company, Trustees Garden was transformed into a fashionable place to live. Along with those residences are the Pirates' House restaurant and the new Charles H. Morris Center, replacing the old shopping village, and what is now parking will soon be garden again.

❧The Haunted Garden?☙

The Morris Center has its own strange stories to tell. Historian Rebecca Clark once owned a gallery on the lower floor of the complex, and she told a tale of a curious and slightly mischievous ghost. "I would come in for work, and the paintings on the wall would all be crooked. At first I didn't think much of it, but it seemed to happen quite a bit, even when I was there. I'd straighten them, and when I would come back by, the picture frames would be cockeyed. Well, one day as I came in, I could see a little boy standing near a painting. As I reached the gallery door I finally saw him do it. He reached out and touched the edge of the frame and knocked it off level, and then he disappeared."

Rebecca smiled when this author asked whether or not she was frightened by this. "Oh please, I'm not afraid of a little boy. He was just curious, and wanted to see the paintings. I just told him not to touch them, and he could stay and look as long as he liked. We got along great after that, and he was very well behaved." She mentioned that she would see the 'boy in blue', as she called him, from time to time, usually out of the corner of her eye.

Rebecca described this boy as being very young, and dressed in late 18th or early 19th century clothing. She had no idea as to his identity, but she theorized from the cut of his clothes that he served on a sailing ship, perhaps even impressed into service by a sailing vessel. This was a frequent occurrence when privateers or other dual purpose merchant warships would run short of able-bodied crewmen. "Perhaps he was taken against his will, and did not survive the voyage," she said sadly. "But he always seemed polite, if a little lonely."

Rebecca does remember a few times he got into trouble with other shopkeepers. "There was a toy store upstairs, and this little boy just couldn't resist. The shop owner had a terrible time keeping toys on the shelves! This would even happen when the owner was there. One moment the toys would be on the shelf, and the next they'd be strewn all over the floor. There was even a morning where the owner was coming into the building to unlock the store, and a ball bounced down the stairs and came to rest at her feet. She said 'somehow' the ball had gotten out of her store and rolled down the stairs. Now, I knew exactly how this had happened, but didn't want to say. The other owner wasn't a big believer in ghosts, you see."

Sometimes boys will be boys, even in the spirit world.

Mulberry Inn

Located on the far east of the city close to the Pirate's House, there sits a structure that has been through many facelifts throughout the years. It now houses the Mulberry Inn, one of the finest hotels in Savannah. Originally built in the 1860's as a livery stable, the building also later served as a cotton warehouse. In the early 1900's, it housed Coca-Cola's first franchise bottling operation. Now fully refurbished as a luxury hotel, the Mulberry Inn offers a glimpse of the city's past, perhaps in more ways than implied by the hotel's glossy brochure.

There are complaints from the front desk that the big grandfather clock in the lobby chimes intermittently. There is one problem with the fact that more than one staff member has claimed to have heard it: the grandfather clock is broken, and is unable to chime at all.

A strange event which has occurred several times first happened in late October of 2000. A staff member received a late-night call at the front desk from room 217, complaining of a strange sound. The couple in 217 had been trying to get some rest and had been awakened by the sound of a horse neighing in an adjoining room. Thinking that a television was simply being played too loudly in an adjoining room, the couple tried to sleep through the noise. After nearly an hour, the exasperated couple could stand it no more, so the front desk was summoned.

The front desk checked the computer and found that no one was staying in rooms to either side of room 217, so two of the staff went up to the hallway to figure out what was going on. Immediately upon stepping out into the hallway, both heard the distinct sound of a horse, whinnying in fear. Halfway down the hallway, one of the pair of workers suddenly decided such an investigation simply was not in her job description. She turned to her co-worker and said, "Tim, I know what I'm hearing, but there's no way there is a horse loose in the hotel. This is not something I'm being paid enough to check out." She refused to go any farther. The other hotel clerk made a thorough check of the hallway, but could find no evidence that the sound was coming from any of the rooms.

The guests were moved to another room in the hotel, and apparently all was well with the rest of their stay. But the question remains: what was the strange sound coming from around room 217? There is the matter of the hotel being the former site of a livery stable (there are records supporting a stable located as late as 1916). The stable partially burned in the 1860's, so perhaps the horses were killed or seriously injured in the fire. It is not uncommon for horses to refuse to leave their stables during a fire, and it has been documented that horses have even been known to run into a burning barn, because they equate their barn with safety. If indeed a horse was killed in this fashion it would certainly explain the strange noises of a horse heard in distress by the guests and the staff.

The staff insists that they have had to deal with this problem numerous times, and are getting tired of 'horsing' around.

In his book, *Behind the Moss Curtain and Other Great Savannah Stories*, fifth-generation Savannahian and local author Murray Silver recounts that the Mulberry was once owned by baseball immortal Shoeless Joe Jackson, who owned a dry cleaning establishment on the corner of Bay and East Broad. Those in search of the ghost of Shoeless Joe have a better chance of finding him here than in Kevin Costner's Iowa cornfield.

Isaiah Davenport House

On the northwest corner of Columbia Square sits the Isaiah Davenport House, a beautiful brick example of Federal-Style architecture. Built on or around 1820, the Davenport House was originally constructed as a private residence, but serves the community today as a house museum. However, according to members of the staff, some of the previous occupants, both two- and four- legged, are still quite comfortable in the house.

The Davenport House stands as not only a jewel of period architecture, it also is a testament of the determination of several prominent Savannahian ladies, who saved the house from demolition in 1955. Their efforts to save the house from the wrecking ball formed the nucleus of the Historic Savannah Foundation, an organization largely responsible for the preservation and conservation of Savannah's Historic District.

Isaiah Davenport was born in Little Compton, Rhode Island in 1784. Little is known about Davenport's early years, though he likely served as a carpenter's apprentice under his father. The Great Fire of 1796 and shipping boom related to the invention of the cotton gin

caused a need in Savannah for experienced carpenters, so when he was twenty-three, Davenport moved to the growing seaport where he began constructing houses as early as 1808. He met Sarah Rosamund Clark shortly thereafter and the two married, with the first of their ten children born in 1810.

Davenport's buildings appealed to conservative Savannahians, and he soon found himself at the head of a successful business. He took on carpenters to help him with various building projects, including fencing around the squares, and constructing numerous homes throughout the city. Davenport bought and sold several lots in the city and grew wealthy enough to own ten slaves.

In 1827, at the age of forty-three, Isaiah Davenport contracted yellow fever and died. He only lived in his beautiful home for seven years. His wife Sarah was a widow at age thirty-nine. She ran a boarding house in the house for a number of years.

Over the years the house served as a private residence and was then sectioned off in the 1890's into apartments, which quickly grew into a tenement house. The condition of the building declined, as did much of the downtown area of Savannah. At one point there were thirteen families living inside the structure!

ᨀHistoric Savannah Foundation is Formed᨟

In 1955, plans were made to raze the structure to make way for a parking lot. A group of seven women fought to save the Davenport House from destruction, and succeeded mere hours before it was scheduled for demolition. It was renovated and finally opened to the public in 1963, quickly becoming one of Savannah's most popular house museums. And as for the Historic Savannah Foundation, what originally began as a women's club with only seven members managed to become one of the most important preservation organizations in the United States.

There have been stories circulating about a previous occupant who appears unwilling to leave the former home, but this former resident is of the feline variety. A spectral orange and white tabby cat (some refer to it as being yellow) has been seen either entering or living within the house, both when this house was a tenement and later as a museum. The museum has a strict no-pet policy, but apparently the rules do not apply to the ghost cat at the Davenport House. The museum has embraced their special four-legged haunting, as there is now a plush ghost cat doll available in the downstairs gift shop. The furtive feline has been seen in several rooms by different members of the staff, often times darting from room to room, and seems to have a special connection to the very young. Children have been known to call a cat that no one else can see, and one child was seen stroking the air, as if petting an unseen kitty cat.

A misty gray vapor has been seen in the gift shop, a shape decidedly human rather than catlike. Also, strange footsteps have been both heard and felt in the downstairs area, as well.

There have also been reports of a little girl in period dress that has been seen playing with a ball on the top floor. She was seen by a tourist, who promptly asked her guide whether the historical reenactors were part of the tour. The tour guide, puzzled, asked her group if anyone else had seen a little girl, and several people on the tour raised their hands. A search for the girl turned up nothing but empty rooms. This same girl has been reportedly seen by tours on the outside of the house—including former Savannah Haunted History tour guide Rhett Coleman in the fall of 2002. "I had just led my tour up to the house, and was about to begin the story of the Davenport House when a woman on my tour pointed to the upper windows. She asked, 'Who is that little girl in the upstairs of the house?'. I turned my head to see, and I did catch a glimpse of white in the window before it, or she, disappeared."

The Davenport House stands as a testament to the preservation and conservation of the city by forward-thinking and concerned citizens. Is it really so farfetched to think that the house, which is tied so intimately into the fabric of downtown's character, could have done some preserving of its own? Perhaps the spirits of those who have passed on have come back to show their approval of Savannah's love of their former home.

The Davenport House, located at 119 Habersham Street, is open to the public:

10 am until 4 pm (last tour begins), Monday through Saturday
1 pm to 4 pm on Sundays

K ehoe House

On the west side of Columbia Square sits the massive Kehoe House, built in 1892 for William Kehoe. The Queen Anne style mansion was built as the Kehoe residence, and it showcased what William was known for in Savannah: iron. What else would the owner of an ironworks foundry use to adorn his house but cast iron railings, Corinthian columns, porches, balconies, and window moldings? The house was built for the sum of $25,000.

William Kehoe is fondly remembered by his granddaughter, Anne C. Rizert, in a November, 1969 issue of the *Savannah News Press Magazine.* She remembered him as "a small person but he stood tall because he had that intangible presence of a man who recognizes his own worth, knowing it was God's graceful gift." She goes on to say that "he was very young when he became involved in the Civil War... he had the misfortune to be poor and on the losing side but this was irrelevant to him. Irishmen always seemed to fight well for lost causes."

Perhaps this poor Irish upbringing explains why he was so fair with his workers. One amusing story involves a worker named Woodrow, who was a 'jack of all trades' for the Kehoe family for many years. Woodrow had a weakness for strong drink which often landed him at the Brown Farm, a now-defunct work farm for misdemeanor offenders. Mr. Kehoe went looking for Woodrow one day at the Brown, and no one was sentenced there by that name. There was, however, someone named 'Kehoe', which of course Woodrow had used as a pseudonym. Rather than being insulted, Kehoe was touched that Woodrow would think enough of him to adopt him.

The Kehoe family was very large—ten children in all. This number may not include stillborn, children who died as infants or very young.

Over the years it was a private residence, but it spent the majority of the 20th century as a funeral home. Today, it is a bed and breakfast, one of the only 4-Star bed and breakfasts in the South, and the only one in Savannah. It is also quite possibly America's only haunted 4-Star establishment.

Tragic End for Twins?

A persistent story, perhaps legend and perhaps not, told about the Kehoe family is that twins were born into the Kehoe family, and that they supposedly died while playing in a chimney in one of the rooms. The fireplaces have all been blocked up, and decorated with angels—perhaps symbolizing the lost children. A series of hauntings have been attributed to these children. Guests on the second floor have often heard children's laughter and small footsteps running down the hall. Some guests have even complained the next morning to the front desk, not realizing that children are strongly discouraged from staying in such a prestigious inn. Even if the rumors of the twins dying in the fireplace are not true, it would not be unusual for the sounds of children's feet running down the halls at the Kehoe House, given the size of the Kehoe clan.

Many of the stories in the house center on the rooms 201 and 203. A guest of room 201 said she awoke in the middle of the night after feeling someone softly stroking her hair and cheek. Thinking that it was her husband, she opened her eyes to find a young child caressing her face—a child who then vanished. No word on whether her screams woke her husband!

In room 203, two sisters had an odd occurrence. One awoke feeling as if someone was sitting next to her. When she opened her eyes, she saw that her sister was sound asleep on the other side of the room, but there was an impression of someone unseen sitting right next to her on the bed.

Even the staff has had some strange incidents. A member of the front desk claims that the doorbell rang one day, even though she could clearly see that no one was there through the beautiful cut-glass door. She ignored this, thinking perhaps that it was a wiring problem. The doorbell rang a second and then a third time. She was about to call for maintenance when suddenly the door unlocked and opened by itself. She found that not only had that happened with the front door, but it had happened to *all the outside doors in the house.* Apparently she was dealing with a ghost that did not like to be kept waiting.

William Kehoe had a weakness for cupolas. His granddaughter Anne theorized that it was perhaps his way of "being the lord of all he surveyed. His cottage at Tybee, his foundry, (and) his home all had one and it was his private preserve for meditation and escape."

This may explain why the cupola's window in the Kehoe House is frequently burning long after dusk. The staff professes no desire to go up into the drafty rafters of the old house, so perhaps it is William, once again feeling like the lord of all creation.

One night a tour guide was passing by the northern side of the Kehoe House with her tour group, and she heard the voice of a little boy, who said, "Play... come play with me." She simply assumed that she was imagining things, until a member of her tour cried out, "Oh my God, did you just hear that?" The guide simply turned back towards her tour and smiled—it was not the first time strange things had happened on one of her tours. All of the tourgoers had heard the disembodied voice of the small boy.

Perhaps the scariest story involving the Kehoe House has nothing to do with ghosts. The house was bought in 1980 by Joe Namath, former New York Jets quarterback (and celebrated pitchman for pantyhose). The persistent rumor is that 'Broadway Joe', as he was called, planned on turning the Kehoe House into nightclub and disco. The residents around Columbia Square voiced an outcry, and the planned nighttime hotspot never materialized. The conservative families around Columbia Square apparently did not have Boogie Fever, and there is a chance they would have turned Joe Namath's nightclub into a Disco Inferno. Burn, baby burn, indeed. However, as an investment for Namath, the house did very well: bought in 1980 for $80,000, the house sold in 1989 for $530,000.

One other chilling point about Kehoe House: they've kept a tradition from when it was a funeral home. The room where breakfast is served each and every morning is still to this day called the Viewing Room.

The Kehoe House is a luxurious 4-Star bed and breakfast. For reservations call (800) 820-1020, or (912) 232-1020. The house is not open for touring.

17Hundred90

At the corner of President & Lincoln St., a wooden Federal-style house holds several of Savannah's most famous ghosts. Built in 1820, the 17Hundred90 Inn and Restaurant pairs a quaint and charming upstairs inn with a superb tavern and restaurant in the downstairs. Why is this structure called the 17Hundred90 when it was built in 1820? Again, history is the answer. No one in Savannah will commemorate the year of 1820 by naming their structure after it because of the terrible tragedies that occurred in that year. Not only did we have a devastating fire, which destroyed two-thirds of the city, we also had a Yellow Fever epidemic in that particular year. Only in Savannah would we have a building called the 17Hundred90 that was built in 1820!

The structure was built in the early part of the 19th century as a boarding house by Steele White, who was a planter from Virginia. Many stories link White with a young servant girl named Anna. Young Anna, as the story goes, was the victim of an arranged marriage, and was forced into both a loveless marriage and a life of near-slave labor. The tales allege that Steele White mistreated her after the two were married. These legends are false, however; Steele White was killed before the house was even completed by a fall from his horse, so Anna and White were never married.

ᨠᕽᨠPersistent Stories᨟ᕽᨠ

Stories involving the supernatural have been told about the 17Hundred90 for as long as anyone can remember, mostly centering on Anna. Different versions of the tale exist, and despite which version you believe, all of these stories share one common theme: Anna plunging to her death from one of her room's windows overlooking a brick courtyard. One version has Anna falling hard, if the pun can be excused, for a married sailor, and committing suicide when he leaves the port city. Another variation has Anna being murdered by her husband, jealous at the obvious attraction between Anna and a young sailor. Yet another has the young servant girl committing suicide when she becomes pregnant by a seaman and he abandons her. Are any of the stories accurate? Did Anna truly meet her tragic end plunging to her death?

According to most of the stories, Anna liked to pick up young men, but in only one instance does this become literal. A waiter named Sean Dunbrook claims to have had a supernatural occurrence in the hallway near the room from which Anna is reputed to have taken her plunge: room 204. He was asked to collect 'B & B cards', or meal cards, off of the doorknobs of the rooms. As he was doing this, he felt a strange sensation. He felt cold, and he also felt as if he were being watched. He went down the third-floor hallway, the feeling growing more and more intense. "Suddenly I felt a force lifting me by my elbows off of the ground," Sean insists. "I looked down and realized that my feet were six inches off of the floor." His next recollection was of running down the hallway, unsure if his feet were even touching the carpet! He says he ran all the way down to the bottom level, running with no regard to his own safety. "To get to the ground floor, I had to run down a small metal spiral staircase. I was running so hard, I nearly flipped over the railing." Sean's tale was certainly hair- (and feet-) raising!

When Sean was interviewed by the Travel Channel, he was asked to conduct the meeting with the film crew in room 204, a request to which he agreed. When he attempted to enter the room, however, he found the doorway to the space inexplicably blocked by an invisible barrier. He paused outside of the doorway, unable to continue forward. The film crew, thinking he was having second thoughts about being on-camera, tried to coax him into the room. Sean had to explain that he literally could not walk into the room because of an impenetrable unseen barrier blocking his path. The film crew had to change their plans, and filmed the segment involving Sean's interview downstairs, instead.

☙Room 204❧

Room 204 has become the center of much of the spectral activity occurring at the 17Hundred90. Management at one time had a waiver form that guests would have to sign in order to stay in the room. The waiver stated that guests who stayed in room 204 would not be issued a refund if they left the Inn abruptly in the middle of the night. The waiver form policy has been discontinued because of the room's incredible popularity with guests, mostly thrill-seekers or amateur ghost hunters. It is quite possibly the most popular room in Savannah, so people wishing to reserve the room for a night's stay are urged to make their reservations far in advance—particularly around Halloween.

Guests who rent the room have reported feeling a feminine presence in the room, and have also reported than Anna likes new technology. She apparently enjoys playing with light switches, even waking some guests out of a sound slumber with her mischievous habit of turning the switches on in the middle of the night. This has been confirmed by many guests who stay in the room, including a man who claimed that the bathroom light kept turning on multiple times—on consecutive nights. In yet another strange instance, a couple staying in the room next door to 204 in May of 2004 claim to have videotaped a mysterious fog in the hallway.

Tour guide Missy Brandt had a couple on tour that was staying in that particular room. They expressed their disbelief in ghosts, but when they got to the 17Hundred90, the woman turned pale. She said, "Before we left to come out on tour, I turned the lights off in the sitting room, bedroom and bathroom." She then pointed towards the windows, which were all ablaze with light. A young man took a digital photograph of the window, and a strange fog is evident in the image, as well as what appears to be a silhouette of a woman looking out of the window.

Anna has also been known, as the story goes, to ransack ladies' bags and remove certain intimate items of apparel. One must remember that if the tales about Anna and sailors are true, she certainly must look her best. Anna will keep the undergarments if she likes them, but if she decides that they are not up to her standards she will return the items.

A couple of ladies from Atlanta visiting close to Christmastime a few years back hadn't heard the stories of Anna's penchant for taking women's undergarments. They left room 204 for a Christmas dinner, and when they returned they found that Anna had removed a few items—and the ladies blamed the staff of the hotel! The staff, trying to calm the women down, offered them a free drink downstairs in the tavern while the misunderstanding was sorted out. The two agreed, but halfway down the stairs leading to the first floor, the woman in the lead let out a scream. From her vantage point on the stairs, she could see the Christmas tree. Anna apparently didn't like these ladies one bit, because she had done a bit of decorating on that tree, using a few 'ornaments' pulled from the women's bags.

∽Another, More Sinister Presence∽

But all is not fun and games at the 17Hundred90. Several swear that there is another more sinister presence, this one in the kitchen. A former owner, Diane Greenfield Smith, claims that when she was in the kitchen on a Sunday afternoon, she felt a hard push in the back and heard a jangle of bracelets. The kitchen and bar staff claims that it is a former cook, an African American woman who was involved in voodoo. Stories abound that she does not like women to invade her kitchen, and will defend it with sometimes terrifying effectiveness.

The maintenance manager was working late one evening, repainting a room. Often times, work can only be done at night, since between the lunch and dinner crowd in the restaurant, and the breakfasts being served for the 'bed & breakfasters' upstairs, the staff has only a small window of time to work in certain areas. So this is how the manager found himself at 3 a.m. at the 17Hundred90 with a paintbrush in his hand. He was all alone, and yet, he heard muffled sobbing coming from the kitchen. He went to investigate, and paused at the kitchen door. The crying was definitely coming from that room, and it was clearly someone not authorized to be in that area. Not having access to a phone, the maintenance manager decided to enter the kitchen. He actually drew a knife to defend himself against the intruder, and walked into an empty kitchen. No one was there, and nothing was amiss—but he did hear a jangle of metal. Perhaps this was the bracelets of the former cook? Deciding the repainting could wait until another time (and when someone else would be there with him), the maintenance man decided to leave as quickly as possible.

A bartender working alone claims that she stepped into the kitchen to investigate the sound of pots clanking together, and suddenly she felt a sting on her ear, almost as if she had been flicked or slapped. Yet another bartender, Lindsay, claims that she has experienced some strange things in the kitchen, as well. Bartenders often have their meals provided by the kitchen. She put in an order for crab cakes one night, one of her favorites and a specialty of the restaurant. Later, she saw her meal waiting on a kitchen table, with the ticket she had written. So she took the meal back up behind the bar and began to eat. The kitchen staff was very angry, because those cakes were intended for a waiting patron of the restaurant. No one remembered seeing an order placed by her, and no ticket was ever found, but Lindsay insists she wrote out the order, and found that ticket right next to her meal. "I saw it with my own two eyes when I walked back there, sitting there next to the plate. This is not the first time this has ever happened, and not just to me. It only happens to the girls that work here, not the men. Whatever the presence is in the kitchen, it hates women."

On another occasion, a bartender expressed her dislike of a certain regular customer. He often insulted her and rummaged with his bare fingers through the fruit trays, a very unsanitary habit. Jokingly, she claimed to put a voodoo hex on him. Less than an hour later, the customer was involved in an accident that seemed to be minor, but he wound up developing complications from the injury, spending considerable time in the hospital. When the bartender was informed that the regular customer was seriously injured, she went very pale and promised not to make light of voodoo at the 17Hundred90— ever. "Maybe the voodoo cook was sending a message," she said between stiff lips.

And the stories continue even right up until the time of this writing. A bartender named Lisa went around to the restaurant side of the building at the end of the night, flipping the switches to turn out the lights at the close of the evening. Lisa could not reach the last switch, and turned away to get a chair to stand on. The light switch behind her flipped off on its own. Lisa stood there for a moment in the dark, considering her next move. Should she run? Finally, she decided that whoever or whatever had turned the light off was trying to be helpful. "Um, thank you," she said, and left the room.

In another instance, one of the servers was asked by a diner if the restaurant was haunted. When she confirmed that yes, it was, the patron said that he had seen a man listening to the piano player who had suddenly disappeared from sight. One moment the man had been leaning against the brick pillars, and the next he had vanished.

One evening, the bartender and a waiter kept hearing unseen children laughing and running through the bar area. The candles on each table which had been lit at the beginning of the night were suddenly blown out by a strange wind which rushed through the area, extinguishing them all. The waiter fled the bar, leaving the poor bartender to fend for herself.

In 2009 I produced a feature-length DVD entitled "Phantoms of History: Savannah," with the intention of developing a series for The History Channel. Three of my favorite sites were chosen for the program and 17Hundred90 was first on my list. The premise for the show is to compare historic fact with haunted fiction and arrive at a fresh conclusion of what happened on site that was of such great impact that elements of the events continue to echo through its hallways today. We not only filmed in room 204, but rented rooms where my producer partner camped. With her was a friend and traveling companion, the mother of a Baptist minister, who did not believe in ghosts— that is, until she awoke one night to find Ana drifting through their suite rumaging through the closet, admiring the ladies' wardrobe.

"Phantoms of History: Savannah" can be found on site at the 17Hundred90 Inn and other inns and shops around Savannah.

Owens-Thomas House

On the northeast side of Oglethorpe Square, the Owens-Thomas House serves as a pinnacle of Savannah architecture, considered by many historians to be the finest example of Regency Style architecture in the United States. Regency Style takes its name from England's King George IV, who ruled as Prince Regent from 1811 to 1820.

Today the Owens-Thomas House has been converted into a house museum. However, there are certain areas of the house that the staff sometimes feels uncomfortable. In Savannah, the dead are never far, and this Regency house is no exception.

Completed in 1819 by 24-year-old architect William Jay, the house is a stunning example of sophistication, both in terms of its fully-realized architectural style and the surprising technology used within. The plumbing system actually featured bathtubs with running water, as well as flushing water closets. The house is constructed of a substance called 'tabby', which is a combination of sand, crushed oyster shells, and lime.

The era of architectural splendor in Savannah started with the completion of the Owens-Thomas House in 1819. William Jay found himself in high demand amongst Savannah's *nouveaux riche*, who were suddenly making fortunes in cotton and exporting. He went on to build the Telfair Mansion (today, the Telfair Museum of Art), the Scarbrough House, and many other buildings that were destroyed over the years, such as a bank, a theatre, and several houses. Jay's involvement is probable, because of Regency-Style influences, in the Wayne-Gordon House, more popularly called the Birthplace of Juliette Gordon Low, and also the old City Hotel on Bay St.

One of the key characteristics of Regency Style is symmetry. The house's interior often contains such quirks as false doors, to satisfy the architecture. Jay also designed a square room in the house to appear round by using visual tricks—again, curved spaces are important to the style, as evidenced as well by the recessed front entrance with a curved door.

Richard Richardson, the original owner of the house, was related to Jay by marriage. Richardson was a banker for the Bank of the United States and a cotton merchant. Three years after the completion of the house, he lost his fortune in the fallout of a failed oceangoing steamship venture, the S.S. Savannah. The house was lost by Richardson when the bank foreclosed. So thus Richard Richardson lost his house when his own bank foreclosed on it!

The house became a prestigious boarding house run by Mary Maxwell, and it was here that the Marquis de Lafayette delivered a speech from the south cast-iron balcony to a group of enthusiastic Savannahians. In 1830, George Owens, congressman and one-time Savannah mayor, purchased the house from the bank for $10,000. It remained in the family until 1951, when Margaret Thomas, Owens' great-granddaughter, bequeathed the house to the Telfair Museum of Art, then called the Academy of Arts & Sciences. Ms. Thomas specified that her room never be altered, and the Telfair has honored her wish.

The Telfair turned the Owens-Thomas House into a museum, which was originally located on the bottom floor, with the upper floors used as apartments. It has been previously reported that one day a spectre made itself apparent to two men who were visiting a friend that lived in the upstairs. The tenant saw nothing, but the two men insist that they saw a man in a riding coat and a shirt with ruffles. The apparition stood in the doorway for a time, then walked through and passed into another room. The two visitors were so flustered by this strange occurrence that they said nothing, and when they asked the tenant if he ever had anything unusual happen, the man simply stated that he was afraid of the downstairs at night. No further visitations of this particular apparition have been reported, however.

The Owens-Thomas House was a favorite location chosen by Robert Redford for his movie "The Conspirator," filmed in Savannah in the fall of 2009 and scheduled for release this year. It is the feel of the place, Redford said, in addition to its visual appeal that makes Savannah the ideal spot to get a glimpse of the past.

ᴄᴏ⋅A Smoking Spirit⋅ᴏᴄ

Tour guide Missy Brandt once related a story involving the exterior cast-iron porch on the southern side of the house museum. She was telling a quick historical anecdote to her ghost tour as they passed by the structure. As she was talking, she heard a match strike behind her and began to smell cigar smoke. She looked around the group and saw that no one was smoking, so she asked if anyone also smelled smoke. "Yes, I saw a match flare up behind you, and smoke puffing out of thin air," a member of her tour group confirmed. This was echoed by several people on her tour, who had all witnessed the phantom match striking in thin air, as well as the cigar smoke, which promptly disappeared when Missy mentioned it.

The carriage house in the back of the property at one time was also the slave quarters. When the upper level was renovated, they found the entire ceiling painted a bright blue color. This is yet another example of 'haint blue', a color that is supposed to repel evil spirits. As detailed in the section devoted to Haint Blue (page 158), it symbolizes water in the Geechee culture, and it is so believed that an evil spirit will not cross water to harm you. The paint was made with a mixture of indigo dye, milk, and lime. This idea of 'haint' blue as a protector may have had a practical value, because the lime would act as a natural insect repellent. Since mosquitoes were the transmitter of Yellow Fever, the Geechee may have stumbled unwittingly into a practice of shielding themselves from one of the most feared diseases

Fever did not extend to the inhabitants of the main house, because Frances Bolton died shortly after the house was completed, and her death is believed to have been from that very illness.

Some workers at the museum are uncomfortable in the carriage house near dusk—with its history of men and women in bondage, it is easy to see why.

In numerous instances, the staff has heard footsteps in both the main house and carriage house at the end of the day. Thinking that some tourists have straggled behind, as sometimes happens, a search will be conducted. Sometimes the staff will find nothing but empty rooms instead of strolling tourgoers. Perhaps the ghosts in the Owens-Thomas House are also busy taking in the beauty and wonders of the house? With William Jay's beautiful design, perhaps that is not so farfetched, after all.

Biblical Ghosts & John Wesley

It is wonderful that five thousand years have now elapsed since the creation of the world, and still it is undecided whether or not there has ever been an instance of the spirit of any person appearing after death. All argument is against it; but all belief is for it.

—James Boswell
Life of Samuel Johnson

In doing research for a book on this subject, one often finds people with religious objections concerning the supernatural. However, the two ideas are not as separate as one might believe. There are even Biblical references to a type of spirituality which closely resembles a modern ghost story:

Matthew 14

²⁶ *And when the disciples saw him walking on the sea, they were troubled, saying, It is a spirit; and they cried out for fear.*

²⁷ *But straightway Jesus spake unto them, saying, Be of good cheer; it is I; be not afraid.*

In this passage, the disciples actually reveal that there is a belief in ghosts during Biblical times. Please note that Jesus seems to take this in stride (no pun intended) and merely puts the disciples at ease, rather than chastising them for believing that he was a 'spirit'.

Matthew 27

⁵⁰ *Jesus, when he had cried again with a loud voice, yielded up the ghost.*

This passage could refer to the Holy Spirit leaving Jesus' body. But there is also the possibility of a personal spirit, meaning Jesus' disembodied soul leaving his body, which later in the text fulfills prophecy by returning:

Luke 24

³⁷ *But they were terrified and affrighted, and supposed that they had seen a spirit.*

³⁸ *And he said unto them, Why are ye troubled? and why do thoughts arise in your hearts?*

³⁹ *Behold my hands and my feet, that it is I myself: handle me, and see; for a spirit hath not flesh and bones, as ye see me have.*

Again, Jesus does not chastise the disciples for believing that he is a spirit. He even notes the difference: he is flesh and blood, whereas a ghost is not. Jesus shows a familiarity with ghosts in this passage which is surprising. His attitude is not anger or derision over the idea that the disciples would think of him as a ghost. Instead he reassures them that it is him, and they can touch his physical body to prove it to themselves if they wish.

The intent of the inclusion of these passages was not to change anyone's stance on religion. It was simply an attempt by the author to leave the door open, and provide an impetus for discussion on the subject. Certainly, other religions have differing views on the subject of the supernatural, most specifically the Geechee culture which still exists in the coastal lowlands of Georgia. The Geechee culture is one that is still fraught with charms, amulets, potions and both white and black magic, and they believe that the dead are all around them at all times.

John Wesley's Unhappy Stay

Also a believer in spirituality of an earthly nature was John Wesley, eventual founder of Methodism. Wesley at first glance would not appear to have a liberal stance on *anything*, much less a Scriptural subject like ghosts.

John Wesley's connection to Savannah was an unhappy one, even though he had a personal invitation. The original pastor in Savannah, Reverend Henry Herbert fell extremely ill, and passage was booked for him to return to England in 1733. In fact, he passed away on the return voyage. James Edward Oglethorpe sent for John and Charles Wesley, whose father had been a trusted friend. They arrived in 1736, but their stay was short in Savannah. Charles fell ill and also fell victim to malicious gossip regarding Oglethorpe, and John ran afoul of trouble in a skirt, namely Sophey Hopkey.

John's strict interpretation of Scripture already made him unpopular—in fact, his stern lectures from the pulpit struck many as too reminiscent of the religious persecution they had fled their Old World countries to escape. But his disastrous handling of Sophey Hopkey's affections would eventually drive him from the colony. Hopkey wanted to marry Wesley, and when he wavered, she married another man. Wesley, slighted, denied the new couple Holy Communion. Wesley was sued for defamation of character, and soon left Savannah in the middle of the night, in the company of a bankrupt constable and a wife beater. His stay in Savannah was a scant 21 months.

'Old Jeffrey'

But John Wesley's early home life in England was dominated by a different kind of spirituality: a household ghost that the family named 'Old Jeffrey'. The ghost in his childhood home had quite an effect on John's spiritual calling to the clergy later in his life.

The ghost would be more akin to a modern-day poltergeist—in this case literally, because the term is German for 'noisy ghost'. And Old Jeffrey was certainly noisy. Tappings, knockings and rappings sounded in the Wesley household, the Epworth Rectory, on a regular basis. Poltergeists have a reputation for inhabiting homes with adolescent children, and this case is no different.

John's mother and father, Susanna and Samuel, were divided on the subject of Old Jeffrey. But the Wesley children regarded the presence as a friend, and the feeling appears mutual. Jeffrey became a favorite playmate of several of the young Wesley children. They would chase his tappings from room to room, and Old Jeffrey would even open doors for the children on occasion.

Susanna was annoyed by Jeffrey, thinking that a playful spirit was essentially wasteful—so much better for all of them if he instructed or warned of danger. But Susanna reluctantly accepted the presence in her home. The Reverend Samuel was more open in his opposition, which caused the spirit to focus on him in a negative way.

Samuel likely made a bad impression when he threatened Jeffrey with a pistol, and had to be persuaded by a close friend that trying to shoot a ghost was impractical, at best. The mischievous Jeffrey would interrupt the Reverend's prayers for King George, causing John later in life to comment on the apparent Stuart leanings of their resident ghost.

Samuel asked the ghost to come to his study, so the two could confront one another. Old Jeffrey responded by pounding out the pastor's own knock he used to signify to his family that he had returned for the day. Jeffrey was clearly mocking the Reverend, and it was just as clear that the Reverend had asked for it. Samuel's study then became a favorite place of Jeffrey's, which had been quiet until that confrontation.

Gradually over time the visitations of Old Jeffrey declined. The Epworth Rectory grew quiet—and one must wonder if it was because the Wesley children grew up. If the spirit known as Old Jeffrey was indeed drawn by the young lifeforce of adolescents, perhaps he grew dormant when they aged. Amazingly, over one hundred years after Jeffrey had so bothered and amused the Wesley family, the rectory once again had a troublesome spirit. The new family was so distraught and troubled by the presence that they moved back to London. Did this family also have many children, with adolescent energy that Jeffrey was drawn to?

✿John's Fascination✿

John Wesley, for his part, was fascinated by the supernatural for the rest of his life. At Oxford, he and brother Charles formed the Holy Club, which investigated reports of paranormal happenings. John, an expert Biblical scholar, understood the scriptural documentation of ghosts, and understood that they were very real. Not only did John have a friend in Jesus, it appears he had a friend in Jeffrey, as well.

One last Savannah tie to John Wesley is his statue erected in the 1970's by sculptor Marshall Dougherty in Reynolds Square. Stories abound of strange orbs and lights caught on digital photos when the subject is the Wesley Monument. Some even claim that it is haunted. However, it is extremely unlikely that John Wesley would haunt his statue, having only spent twenty-two months here. However, there are signs that the rocky relationship between Savannah and Wesley are being repaired, judging by how often devious Savannahians surreptitiously slip a plastic cup of beer into John Wesley's outstretched hand. So, in this way, perhaps the monument is imbued with 'spirits', after all.

Jumper on Drayton Street

An imposing office building on Drayton Street has, if the story is to be believed, a tale with a real impact on the listener. The Realty Building, built in 1921, is one of the structures that dominate Savannah's skyline. This ghost tale is more than likely a bit of folklore cooked up to scare employees, primarily new members of the night janitorial crew. Several different versions exist. The story is recounted here as just a legend, and should be treated as such, but is such an entertaining story that it was included in this volume.

October 29th, 1929 was Black Tuesday, the Great Crash, or the start of the Great Depression. People all over the world lost their fortunes on that day, and a number of people also took their own lives. As the story goes, one of those suicides happened at the Realty Building. A gentleman who was working late had lost his fortune and decided to take his own life. He did it correctly, because he jumped from the top floor, and hit Drayton St. at an estimated 85 mph.

Flash forward to late October, 1969. We had a young gentleman just starting his new job as a janitor. He was working late, and was all alone on that top floor, cleaning up. Suddenly he saw another man step out of an *empty* office he had just cleaned. This man loosened his collar, took off his hat, and walked to one of those middle two windows, and jumped to his death. The janitor was alarmed, and called the Savannah Police Department. Two squad cars and an ambulance raced down to the foot of the Realty Building, but were surprised to find *no body* on Drayton St. The police went up and had a talk with that janitor about phoning in false emergencies.

That following evening, that same janitor was cleaning up all alone on that top floor. Suddenly, he saw the same man step out of the same office. He loosened that same collar, took off that same hat, opened one of those middle two windows, and jumped to his death yet again. Now, that janitor was a very practical man: he didn't call the police again. He understood that what he was seeing was a spirit. He was also practical because of what he brought with him that following night to work: *a hammer and a nail*. And he tried to fix this problem by nailing that window shut.

So, working that third evening in a row, this janitor was eager to see if that gentleman would return. He didn't have to wait long, because once again he stepped into that hallway. Once more that man loosened his collar, took off his hat, and walked to that nailed-shut window. Imagine the look of surprise on the janitor's face when that window opened right up, and that man jumped to his death once again. The reason that window opened is because this man is reliving the same moment of his death in 1929. That nail wasn't in the window in 1929, so it will never be nailed shut for this gentleman.

over the years, by numerous
rical staff that work in this
st years, and he's also seen
ck Market takes a little dip.
ial advice is that if you hear
't late October and you own

a man on tour began to look
ed him if anything was the
as fine, but I was still worried
that nothing was the matter,
nnah to start a new job, and
o he wanted to take a walking
told me, "The problem is that
in the building at which you
were just po......... top floor!"

Lucas Theatre

The Lucas Theatre was built in 1921 by Arthur Lucas at the corner of Abercorn and Congress Streets, on the southeastern edge of Reynolds Square. The beautiful theatre, with an Italian Renaissance exterior and fully- renovated interior, is an edifice responsible for improving and enriching the cultural atmosphere of this unique Southern city. The theatre remained open until 1976, and the last movie that showed before the doors were closed was The Exorcist. A number of people tried to renovate the Lucas during its vacancy. Even actor Kevin Spacey, who was in town filming *Midnight in the Garden of Good and Evil*, gave a sizeable donation and hosted a black-tie fundraiser. The grand old theatre finally reopened its doors in December of 2000, with a showing of *Gone with the Wind*.

But this tribute to the arts in Savannah has also had its share of ghost stories throughout the years, some true, and some with their veracity very much in doubt, but they are colorful tales nonetheless.

One bit of folklore being told as fact about the structure is the claim that in 1928, a group of gangsters in a car opened fire on a crowd of people waiting to get into the Lucas Theatre with a .45 caliber Tommy Gun. Some point to a grouping of blackened marks on the outside of the Lucas' tile façade as evidence of the repair job done to hide the bullet holes. The story continues, claiming that a ticket-taker was shot in the back by these men as he attempted to reach safety within the doors of the theatre. Claims of seeing this man abound, who supposedly flings open the front doors, staggers into the movie-house lobby, falls to the floor, and vanishes from sight.

The first problem with this story is that the shooting never happened. No incidents of a drive-by shooting have ever taken place at the Lucas Theatre. An exhaustive search of the archives at the Georgia Historical Society reveal not one bit of supporting evidence for this story. Also, since the box office was located inside, the ticket-taker would have been stationed inside the lobby next to the main doors leading into the theatre, not on the sidewalk. And lastly, the black marks pointed to by tour guides are decidedly not caused by .45 caliber bullets. A round from a Thompson machinegun would have almost certainly shattered the Spanish-style tile, or at the very least left a gaping hole, not left the dark smudges that are apparent on the front of the Lucas.

⌒The $10,000 Haunting⌒

But there are some strange stories about the Lucas which have the ring of truth.

A longtime Lucas Theatre executive, Jon Leisure, told this author a story that occurred fairly close to the completion of the theatre: "We were getting ready for the premiere in December of 2000, and one of the problems we were having was that the air conditioners located above the balcony were leaking water. So we rigged up what we thought was a solution. We strapped what amounted to a funnel on the underside of the a/c unit, so the dripping water would flow into the funnel, down a hose and into a 5-gallon bucket at the bottom." John went on to say that the plastic lid of the bucket was left on, and the hose passed through a small hole which was cut into the lid. The fit had been so tight, he insisted, that it had taken some 'elbow-grease' to get the hose through the hole in the first place. "It was a snug fit," he said, shaking his head.

"When we came back the next morning, the hose was no longer in the bucket. Somehow, the hose had been pulled out of the hole in the lid. There was no way that hose could have gotten out of the bucket unless somebody pulled it, hard!

"The dripping water had absolutely ruined a portion of the balcony, an area that had recently been finished. It cost nearly $10,000 worth of damage to the plaster. Fortunately, it didn't affect the premiere."

Several of the workers involved in the renovation also claim to have had an otherworldly experience. One worker reported hearing the sound of a whirring projector and a light coming from the old projection booth. The problem was, it was early in the renovations and the projector had not yet been re-installed in the projection room.

But the ghost stories predate the renovation. One former employee who worked at the Lucas in the early '70's remembers an incident. "We were all pretty sure the place was haunted—even back then there were stories," he said. "But boys being boys, we would often use this to scare some of the female employees, by hiding and jumping out, that sort of stuff.

"Well, one day it backfired. I hid in a dark room, ready to spring out and scare one of the girls, when suddenly I felt a presence in there with me. I could hear someone there in the dark, in the room with me. I knew I was all alone in there, but I could also feel them watching me. I made a pretty quick exit, and I also lost my enthusiasm for hiding in dark corners at the Lucas Theatre."

Other members of the staff have reported hearing applause coming from the empty theatre. "I was walking into the theatre to start my shift," one former employee recalls, "and I hear what sounded like a full theatre applauding. I remember thinking that it was odd, because it was early afternoon before the movies really got busy—why would there be a full audience watching a matinee, and why would they applaud? I walked to the door of the movie theatre and opened it, and it was deserted. We hadn't been showing a matinee at all."

It is only fitting that such a cornerstone of Savannah's culture throughout the years would also have another type of deep connection to Savannah's past. The stories of things that go bump in the night at the Lucas are perhaps exposing the 'reel' side of this beautiful Southern town.

ᴄᴏ~An Apt Showing~ᴏᴄ

The very first movie shown at the Lucas Theatre was a 1921 film called *Camille,* based on a play by Dumas. In it, the title character falls deeply in love with a young man, but circumstances intercede and the two part ways. After hard luck, the two lovers are reunited, and find that their love for each other is still strong.

This film could be a metaphor symbolizing our two lovers: the Lucas Theatre and the city of Savannah, reunited at last.

Marshall House

Unlike so many structures in Savannah that have been converted into rooms for rent later in their life, this was built originally to be a hotel, and has been used for that purpose for most of its history. The hotel is considered to be one of the finest structures Mary Marshall ever built. The beautiful Greek Revival hotel sits on Broughton St., but the exterior is evocative of something more commonly expected in the French Quarter of New Orleans, complete with a cast iron verandah. The upscale hotel boasts a fully-appointed bar, an adjoining fine-dining restaurant, and a front lobby which gleams of marble.

The Marshall House Hotel was built in 1851 by Mary Marshall. Her father, Gabriel Lever, a 19th century cabinet maker, bought some property on Broughton Street and passed it on to his daughter when he died. Mary built the hotel on the site, and it is considered by architectural historians to be the finest structure she had built in

Savannah. The cast iron balconies and verandah were added in 1857. Years later, the hotel changed ownership and was renamed the Geiger Hotel, after its new proprietor, Minnie Geiger. In 1933, Herbert W. Gilbert leased the hotel and changed its name to the Gilbert Hotel, which closed in September 1945.

The hotel was reopened again as the Marshall Hotel in 1946 after extensive renovations. When their 10-year lease ran out in 1956, the owners decided it cost too much to bring the building up to the standards required by Georgia fire codes. The hotel closed, and many thought it would be the last time. But the Marshall House underwent extensive renovations in 1999 and re-opened its doors to the public as a luxury hotel.

❧Haunted Happenings on Broughton Street❧

Otherworldly stories persist about the Marshall House. Before the hotel reopened in August of 1999, the staff reported strange odors and something that can only be described as "bad vibes" from rooms 214, 314, and 414. Many different types of deodorizers were used, to no avail, and even an ozone machine was tried without success. Finally, the staff tried something drastic: group prayer. This worked nearly immediately in rooms 214 and 314, but 414 was different. That particular room had an aura and odor so oppressive that the staff members could not stay in the room long enough to pray. Finally, the housekeeping manager fixed on a unique solution: a radio tuned to a gospel station was placed in the room, with the volume turned up. This apparently worked, since both the odor and strange menacing vibes have not been experienced since.

Some staff members and guests alike have reported hearing the sounds of a small child bouncing a ball up and down the upper hallways of the hotel. Many hotel guests have asked about the disembodied sounds of the pitter-patter of a child's feet in the halls, or of a child laughing. Others still have reported seeing a spectral cat, which then vanishes.

One former bartender claims that he heard the sounds of footsteps many times over the bar when he knew that area was deserted. He even heard a rhythmic banging sound coming from over the bar that had several people smiling into their hands. "It sounded like a couple was up there trying to break the bed, so to speak," Kevin said with a wink, and the implication was clear. When he mentioned it to the front desk staff, they informed him that the room directly above the bar was empty.

A physician and his wife mentioned an encounter with the Other Side at checkout one morning. It seems the doctor had been awakened several times by a gentle tickling sensation on his feet in the middle of the night. In his sleepy state he was convinced that the comforter or the sheets were somehow responsible for the sensation of something lightly brushing his feet. The last time it occurred, he looked down to see a little girl tickling his feet. She smiled and vanished.

Some have had the chilling sensation of awakening to feel a hand being pressed against the guest's forehead, exactly like someone was taking their temperature. Some research turned up the fact that for a time during the War Between the States, the Marshall House was used by the Union Army as a hospital. Sherman's troops occupied the hotel and the Union army turned it into a hospital until the war ended, some six months later. Perhaps the former medical staff at the Marshall House is still fulfilling their duty to care for the occupants of the rooms, not realizing the conflict is long-since over, and the people tucked into their beds at night are not in need of medical treatment.

☞A Terrible Discovery☜

This link to being a medical facility would also explain why, when the Marshall House underwent renovations in the late 1990's, the workers made a grisly discovery in a downstairs room. Some floorboards had rotted, and were in need of replacement. When they pried up the floorboards, they found human remains. When the authorities were called in, they treated is as if it were a crime scene, carefully cataloguing the remains they were finding. The odd thing about it was that they were finding hands, feet, arms and legs. Some tests revealed that the body parts dated from the Civil War era, thus confirming their Union connection.

The downstairs was used as a surgery, and a number of amputations were performed in that room. A surgical procedure such as removal of a gangrenous limb was performed very differently than it is today. Anesthesia was in short supply. The unfortunate soldier had to be held down by strong hands, and the offending limb was sawed off. Doctors are nicknamed 'Sawbones' even today because of this gruesome practice. The average amputation took less than a minute. The wound was then packed with sawdust or lint with no regard for sanitary or antiseptic surgery. Also in use during that time period was the practice of placing a lead bullet between the teeth of the soldier receiving the amputation, giving the poor soul something to bite on during the crude procedure. This gives rise to the phrase 'bite the bullet'. With that origin is it any wonder that the saying means doing something very much against one's will?

With the severed limbs piling up, the Union soldiers found a quick and easy way to be rid of the leftover body parts: they pulled up a floorboard or two and tossed the severed body parts under the floor. There were several groupings of limbs, presumably because the surgeons would bury each day's amputations in a bundle together.

In an ordinary year, the smell would have been horrendous. But the winter of 1864 was one of the coldest winters Savannah's ever had on record, so those body parts would have decomposed slowly, and the Marshall House was abandoned for many years after Sherman's troops left town. So there these body parts remained—until 1999! The Union soldiers left Savannah a souvenir that wasn't found until 135 years later.

Here is where Savannah's morbid sense of humor kicks in: what better room to use as a night manager's office? Managers have complained of strange noises emanating in or around that office. Low moans and strange unexplained footsteps have been heard. One manager saw a shadowy figure pass by the open door to the office, and this happened at a time that he was supposedly alone. The man was wearing a heavy dark blue overcoat. He also claimed that there was one other odd thing about the man that he saw—the fact that he only had one arm. This Union soldier has been seen on numerous occasions.

When the human remains were removed from the office, the strange noises immediately started. The ghosts apparently miss their severed limbs, and have begun to search for them. One can only suppose that the Marshall House charged those Union soldiers an arm and a leg for their stay.

One manager had many problems sorting through her paperwork in the downstairs. She would find that documents she had just organized would be out of sequence moments later, papers would switch stacks on her by themselves and throw off her totals, and stacks of cash would mysteriously reorganize themselves. Exasperated, she had to admonish the ghost. "Okay, I don't mind your playfulness, I like fun and games," she said aloud. "I know I'm sharing your space, but please don't play with the money." The paranormal activity in the office, she claims, became drastically less frequent from that moment on.

At least for her. One security guard confirmed that there was definitely something odd about the downstairs. "There are some weird sounds down there, and they're not being made by the elevator," he said, cryptically. When pressed as to what he has heard on the lower level, he simply said, "Sounds that shouldn't be there."

◦◦A Ghost Story with Real Bite◦◦

Another terrifying incident seemingly straight out of the movie *The Shining* occurred in room 304. A mother and her preschool-aged daughter were staying in the room one night, and the mother was in the sitting area reading while the daughter was in the bathroom. The mother became aware that she could hear her daughter speaking, but even more disturbing was the fact that she could hear *two* voices, and it wasn't the television. Her daughter sounded agitated. She asked her daughter who she was talking to, and her little girl responded, "The little boy in the bathtub." When she walked into the bathroom, wondering who on earth was in the bathroom with her daughter, she found her girl in near tears, pointing to an empty bathtub. The girl said, "He's right there and he has big teeth and he bit me!" The girl did indeed have a bite mark complete with teeth impressions on her arm, just above her elbow on the *back* of her arm. It was in an area that her daughter would have no way of reaching with her own mouth, let alone biting. Needless to say, the pair was given a new room at a new hotel, free of charge, no questions asked.

This is not the only incident of strange bites at the hotel. Another woman, a Director of Sales for a prominent company, who stayed in a nearby room reported waking up with a bite mark on her arm. It appeared to be a child's bite, and it was done with enough force to leave a bruise on her skin. This was found on her upper inner arm, in an area nearly impossible to reach on oneself without being a contortionist. Even stranger (or perhaps more telling of the amenities at the Marshall House), the woman still continues to stay at the hotel while on business trips to Savannah. Perhaps, then, she was bitten by Savannah's charm, as well.

The Strange Case of Charles C. Jones, Jr.

There is no present...
And no future;
There is only the past,
Brittle with relics.

—R.S. Thomas
Welsh Landscape

Historian Colin Young related the following tale, one involving one of Savannah's most prominent men during the latter half of the 19th century:

Many ghost stories are dismissed as imaginings of simple minds. But one tale that refuses to be dismissed as such is the story of Charles Coldcock Jones, Jr. He was a well-respected Savannahian and one of the brightest men of his era. During his life he was a Harvard graduate, artillery officer for the Confederacy, prominent attorney, published author, historian, and also the mayor of Savannah. He was also a believer in ghosts—at least after living in a townhouse close to the intersection of State & Bull Streets.

According to Colin, who actually has played the character of Charles Jones Jr. for his Lantern Tour in Laurel Grove Cemetery, young Charles was working late one night on a difficult case. It seemed that a woman named Miss Jane had been duped into marriage by a young widower, who demanded that she sign a will handing over all of her property to his children. Needless to say, the marriage was not a happy one. She died, and her relatives in Charleston hired Charles to represent them in the fight to overturn the will. This was complicated by the fact that after Miss Jane passed away, Charles rented the very home that she and her argumentative young widower had formerly been living. So Charles found himself living in the late Miss Jane's house, representing her family against his own landlord.

The night before the case was to be argued, Charles worked long into the night. He sat at the dining room table with his law books and a cigar. From the hallway he heard light footsteps, and a woman walked into the dining room. She was an utter stranger. She was pale, thin, and wore a mourning gown. She seemed to be in the throes of absolute sadness, and devoid of life. She walked with her head down, plodding past him into the dark parlor. Charles thought at first that he was dealing with someone mentally confused who had wandered in—being a Southern gentleman, he called out to see if he could be of assistance. When he got no answer, he rose from his chair, took the light from the table, and followed. But he found himself all alone in the parlor. The woman had entirely vanished.

Young Charles sat back at his table, wondering if he had dreamed the woman, but found that his cigar was still burning, and the ink on his legal papers was still wet. The most unusual part of the whole experience was that he had both seen *and heard* his apparition.

Charles won the case for the Charleston heirs the following morning. Later, he discussed his strange late-night experience with a neighbor. He described the woman he had seen, and the neighbor went suddenly pale. She asked if the apparition was wearing a mourning gown. When he said yes, the neighbor said words that chilled Charles Jones to the bone:

"That description sounds exactly like Miss Jane."

Was this the ghost of the unhappy woman? If so, apparently Miss Jane was more than happy with Charles' hard-won settlement for her family, because she never troubled him again. In fact, the apparition has never troubled anyone else at that location, either, proving that sometimes the just application of the law can even make the spirits happy.

The incident where Charles encountered a spirit is notable because of the fact that such a learned man would be so forthright and open regarding his brush with the supernatural.

The Anonymous Bar

Many times, a problem that a ghost researcher often encounters are owners of businesses with an agenda. Embellishing a tale to draw in business sometimes occurs, but several owners have flat-out stated that "creativity" is better than historical accuracy—the owner of a pub or tavern, for example, is eager for the tours to include their establishment on the route. Ringing cash registers, no doubt, drown out any inner complaints of conscience.

Conversely, the opposite also occurs. Undoubtedly rare, the occasion arises where a proprietor with genuine phenomena wishes to distance him or herself from the added exposure or publicity associated with ghost stories. Reasons for this vary, and one case in point is a bar located in Savannah which will have to go unnamed, at the ownership's request. You, Good Reader, will have to figure out the identity of this establishment on your own—the clues are here, for those who can read between the lines.

Located in the heart of the Historic District, this recently renovated structure was built after the Civil War. One of several former warehouses, the building has found new life as an elegant and stylish nightclub. Under that debonair exterior, however, lurks one of the most terrifying stories this author has ever heard.

Not only is the structure haunted by ghosts—stories like the ones with which this volume is brimming—but there is also a presence or force at work which is so malevolent that several staff members and co-owners have fallen prey, with serious and life-threatening consequences. Ghosts don't generally send the staff to the hospital, as happened in several instances in this bar, whose name, lamentably, I cannot mention. Eerie forces are, or were, at work in the structure, at least as related by a former owner and good friend of the current management, as well as a good friend of this author.

ঔ৽Strange Happenings৽ঔ

"I was there once with my brother, in the basement," the former owner told me one night over a drink, "And the upstairs was deserted. I had just gotten there, and my brother had been downstairs working for hours before I showed up. While we're down there renovating the place, I hear heavy footsteps running across the floor above me, y'know, *bump bump bump!* I'm looking around, because the place is deserted—who the heck is upstairs? Well, my brother barely looks up even though we're the only two there. He says, 'Man, that's been driving me nuts.' So I asked him, 'Why, who is it up there?', and he just looks at me and says, 'Nobody. It's deserted'. My brother took a long drag of his cigarette, like he's thinking about whether or not he should finish what he was saying. I guess he decided to, because he said, 'I've been hearing it all night and when I've gone up to check, I didn't find anybody. *We're alone.*'" The former owner grew very solemn as he talked. "My brother is not the sort of guy who makes stuff up. He is a pretty literal person, and a very hard worker. We both heard it, and it was footsteps. It wasn't any settling floorboard or mouse; these were heavy stomps coming from a deserted space above us.

"We actually heard that pretty frequently. Footsteps, voices, that sort of thing. There were times, like that instance with my brother, where more than one person would hear it."

This author has heard many haunted stories about that city block, and one common theme is that someone died in a fire. And indeed, one of the largest threats to Savannah during that time period was fire. Many of the large blazes which have plagued the city have started in that area, including one of the worst fires in Savannah's history, the Hogan's Dry Good Fire of 1889. Are these the ghostly footsteps of someone who perhaps died in one of the conflagrations?

ঔ৽A Dark Turn৽ঔ

One other story told by the former owner about the space sent chills down this author's spine—possibly because of the subject matter, or possibly the fact that it had such a profound impact on the life of my friend. In fact, it nearly killed him.

"So the renovations are complete, and the bar opens," he continued. "The problem is, people that worked there were having accidents or medical problems. I worked behind the bar, and one day I keeled over and had to go to the emergency room. Turns out, I almost died. I still have a soft spot in my skull from the surgery, want to feel it?" At this point he offered to let me touch his soft spot, an honor I declined. "It wasn't just me. In eight weeks we had ten people nearly die or had emergency-room-type injuries. We had a broken leg and an auto accident, that sort of thing. My brother nearly wound up in the same room as me at the hospital. There were others.

"One day I'm back behind the bar, still not really recovered from my surgery, and I'm talking to my brother, just basically saying how weird it is that so many people have been hurt in such a short amount of time. And my brother, real casual, says, 'Do you think maybe that Pentagram drawn in the upstairs has anything to do with it?'

"I nearly fell over. I said, 'WHAAAT?', and he showed me. There was a big Satanic symbol, a Pentagram drawn in black on the upstairs floor—and it was *right above the bar!* Everyone who had been hurt was working right underneath that big 'hex' sign, and didn't even know it. A big symbol, and black candles, the whole bit. My brother and I erased the drawing, and the problems stopped right away."

The symbol, most associated with black magic or Satanism today, has roots in many religions, but I was not about to quibble semantics with my friend. After all, *he* was the one with a soft spot in his skull, not I. It does stand to reason that the symbol above the bar was used in some sort of dark, forbidden, malevolent ritual, as opposed to a Wiccan ceremony, or even the Freemasons.

The ghost stories regarding the bar are not unusual, but the Occult symbol and what was possibly a Satanic ritual by persons unknown is an extraordinary and disturbing twist. Were the owners and staff the target of a curse? And what was the motivation? The question remains unanswered, and the bar must remain unidentified by request of all of the parties involved.

Is it a coincidence that all the stories associated with the bar involve fire? The block has been destroyed by fire numerous times in the early days of Savannah—quite possibly spurring a haunting— and now the owners and staff have had to deal with a different sort of incident, also involving fiery torment. One hopes that *all* such flames have been extinguished at this location.

B&B Billiards

On Congress Street near Bay there sits a unique 'L'-shaped building with a storied past. Its myriad uses are indicative of Savannah's ever-changing role as a seaport. Currently home to B & B Billiards, the finest billiards hall in Savannah, the structure has reflected the shifting fortunes and financial tides of this unique Southern city. The building is also the site of some rumored tragedy, and like so many edifices in this coastal Georgia town, it has a haunted reputation.

The structure's history was difficult to uncover. A year-by-year search of the city directory finally shed some light on the many uses of the current home to B & B. Even the building offers conflicting clues: listed as being built in 1860, it appears to date from an earlier time. The foundation appears much older than the current edifice, being made from a different brick—Savannah Grey bricks instead of the red brick used to build the old warehouse. It was a grocery store in the 1890's, and was also at various times a dry goods store, a shoemaker's shop, a carriage and wagon shop, a tinner, and a shop which produced manual sewing machines. It was a factory owned by International Harvester shortly before the 1930's, and was vacant throughout the Great Depression. After being empty for a time, it was home to the Chatham Shoe Company, an Indian Motorcycle franchise, and a furniture company.

Often times the research can paint a pretty accurate picture of more than just the history of the structure. I began to get a feel of the changing uses of this area—as Savannah grew, so did the surrounding buildings. What was once a low-income residential area off to the west became more industrial, and the grocers and shoemakers gave way to companies like International Harvester and Indian Motorcycles. In more modern times, the city changed again, and these mechanical companies have given way to tourist-geared enterprises: bars, nightclubs and restaurants.

The current owners, Caitlin and Craig, graciously agreed to be interviewed for this volume. This author quickly came to the conclusion that they were seeking answers—several supernatural incidents had happened to them directly, and their motivation was to find out with *whom* or *what* they were dealing. This was not a desire to be included in the ghost-tour trade, it was personal. The strange occurrences had not only involved them, but the staff had also been affected, as well as their own family.

They bought the structure in 2001, and almost immediately, the strange incidents began to occur. The previous owner had claimed that the place was haunted, but Craig did not believe in ghosts. He smiled politely as the woman related several stories, but he felt such tales were ridiculous. The woman added that there had been an accident in the downstairs: the police department had at one time used the area as a shooting range, and one of the young officers was mortally injured. The man's name, she said, was Charlie, and they shouldn't be surprised if Charlie showed up now and again.

This author did a thorough search of the records and found no such incident chronicled, and also found no references to the structure ever being used as a shooting range by the police. The lack of documentary evidence, however, does not mean it did not happen. In fact, the far western wall is riddled with bullet holes, including several slugs embedded in the pockmarked brick. It is entirely possible that it was an informal arrangement with an owner—perhaps a friend of the officers? Perhaps it was even used for such a purpose when it was vacant. The evidence to support the woman's story is literally wedged in the bricks, and there is further evidence—if the story of Charlie is to be believed.

Some Strange Encounters

Caitlin has had several encounters with Charlie. She was painting the floor one day, and felt a presence over her shoulder. She glanced briefly, more of just a flick of her eyes to confirm that someone was there, and continued painting. She began talking to the person—whom she assumed to be Craig—and only turned around when she got no answer. There was no one behind her. She described the man whom she had seen as a tall man in a hat, but her attention had been on the floor so she got no better look at him.

A former employee named Ginger is also said to have had an experience with Charlie. She walked in one afternoon before B & B had opened, and spotted a man she had never seen before. He was sitting at the bar, wearing a wide-brimmed hat, a tan shirt and pants, and boots. He then disappeared.

A former cook, nicknamed Fluffy, was terrified of the downstairs space. "He was one of those guys who look absolutely ferocious," Caitlin explained, "But underneath his tattooed and pierced Goth exterior, he was an absolute sweetheart. He was also very afraid of ghosts." One day Fluffy came out of the kitchen looking very pale, or at least paler than usual. He announced that he would not cook in the kitchen by himself, and the only reason he gave was that it was haunted. Fluffy would not elaborate, and he also never worked a shift alone again.

A humorous happening involving two couches, apparently unrelated to Charlie, occurred shortly after the club opened. The 1950's-era couches had been placed in the downstairs, and one day a distributor who was making a delivery asked about "the woman in the beehive hairdo who was sitting all alone in the downstairs on the couch." The couches were removed, and the woman was never seen again.

Craig, a non-believer in ghosts until his numerous experiences at B & B, came in early one morning. He found every light left burning in the bar, all four burners on the stove set to 'high', and the stereo full-blast with a CD skipping. Craig, after turning everything off, made a call to the manager who had worked the night before, and asked him why he had left everything on. The manager professed ignorance, and only then did it occur to Craig that it would be difficult to leave all of those implements running and not notice—especially the stereo, which was oddly skipping on a CD that in all other instances had worked just fine. "I mean, who would leave the stereo on full-blast?"

"If you've worked here for any period of time, you believe," Craig related. He then told a story involving the stairs. He was walking into the downstairs, where he spotted a puddle on one of the wooden steps. "This wasn't a puddle which had splattered; it was a perfectly round puddle which looked like someone had taken a pitcher and poured it out at a low height. I thought that I had better clean it before someone slipped, so I grabbed a hand-towel off the bar and walked back. The puddle *was gone.* I don't mean cleaned up or drained away, I mean the stairs were completely bone-dry, all of them." He shook his head. "Either I'm crazy, or..."

Sometimes, the ghosts can be friendly or helpful. One day, Craig was doing some paperwork at the bar. He suddenly realized that he needed a pen, when one suddenly clattered down in front of him on the metal bar top. It fell, he said, with pretty good velocity, like it had been dropped from the ceiling. He looked around, thinking someone was playing a prank on him. The bar was deserted except for him, however.

Supernatural Photos

In another instance, Craig's young daughter was in the downstairs before B& B opened. She had never played billiards before, so instead of using the pool cue to 'shoot' at balls, she was using it to rake balls into pockets. Craig saw this and thought it would make a cute picture, so he started snapping with his digital camera. All of the photos but two turned out crystal-clear, with nothing out of the ordinary. But those two photos reveal something extraordinary: what appears to be tendrils of strange mist or fog enveloping her. Craig is not a smoker, and the downstairs was deserted, so the odd mist is not cigarette smoke. Craig insists that there was nothing amiss when he started taking the photos. "Look on one of the photographs," Caitlin points out, "the mist is surrounding her arm, almost as if whatever is surrounding her is helping her."

Perhaps with enough research, the story of 'Charlie' will eventually come to light. Will the supernatural occurrences cease when Charlie's true story is told? One can never tell. Until then, Craig and Caitlin will have to find a way to live in peaceful co-existence with their spirit. Fortunately, it does not appear to be a malevolent presence. Punctuating the sharp crack of billiard balls being put into play at B & B is the occasional strange apparition, or ball-point pen being delivered by unseen hands. Charlie's motivation is as yet unknown in this favorite Savannah nightspot, where 'shots' has a triple meaning. Shots of alcohol are served at the bar, patrons playing billiards take their shots in convivial games—and gunshots, fired long ago, the impact of which perhaps is still being felt today.

B & B Billiards: 411 West Congress Street, (912) 233-7116 featuring billiards, exotic beers, and a late-night full-service menu. Hours are 4 pm to 3 am everyday except Sunday (1 pm to 2 am).

Scarbrough House

The beautiful Regency mansion on Martin Luther King Blvd., which now houses the Ships of the Sea Maritime Museum, was built for William Scarbrough in 1818. The historic home was built by William Jay for perhaps the leading Savannah merchant of the time period.

The house has a historic past: U.S. President James Monroe was entertained here in 1819, when he had made a special trip to witness the launching of the *S.S. Savannah*, the world's first oceangoing steamship. Scarbrough was a principal investor in the venture. Scarbrough proudly invited Monroe and other dignitaries to his newly completed home before the ship set sail to England.

The voyage of the *S.S. Savannah* was a rousing success on the high seas, where she set a record for fastest journey across the Atlantic. Unfortunately, she was an abject failure where it really mattered: the bottom line of the ledger. The steamship was not a financial success and the investors lost a fortune. Scarbrough was ruined in the fallout, and he was forced to sell his lovely home at auction. It was bought by William's son-in-law, who allowed William to continue to live at the residence.

Perhaps contributing to the financial debacle was the fact that William's wife, Julia, was especially fond of parties, or 'blowouts', as she called them. She was dubbed 'The Countess', and she once sent out five hundred invitations for a single party—three hundred wound up attending. These 'blowouts' were nearly unceasing. One lady visitor to Savannah wrote: "We hear ladies with families of small children boast of having been out to parties 10 nights in succession until after midnight, and sometimes until 3 o'clock in the morning; and that they had not seen their husbands in a week." Robert Mackay, a friend of Julia's, did warn that her skill as a hostess did nothing for her skill as a singer, and that she not be asked to sing lest she "frighten the good people of England."

In intervening years between the Scarbrough (and extended) family's ownership and 1997, when the Maritime Museum began occupying the structure, the mansion was used as an orphanage, a school for African-American children, and as a museum by the Historic Savannah Foundation. The house for years was allowed to slide into disrepair and then ruin before the HSF restored it over many years.

But even though the blowouts thrown by Julia Scarbrough had ended years before, that doesn't stop many longtime Savannahians from talking about the house. Some claim to have seen the windows ablaze in the mid-Sixties, when the house was unoccupied. According to these accounts, the sounds of laughter and raucous piano music have been heard coming from the house in the wee hours of the morning. Perhaps 'The Countess' was so fond of parties that she continued to throw her grand 'blowouts' well into the next century.

ᴗ☜Brothers, & Armed?☞ᴥ

A family legend that involves the younger Julia Scarbrough, daughter of William and Julia, is one in which her eventual husband, Godfrey Barnsley, fought an unusual duel with his own brother, Gartrelle. It seems that they both loved the same woman, a young lady named Chessie Scarlett. Unable to settle who should have her hand in marriage, the two siblings decided the fight a 'poison duel' to decide the matter. They arranged for an impartial friend to pour two glasses of wine, and into one was added a lethal dose of poison. The appearance and character of the wine was unchanged, so neither had any way of telling which glass held just the spirits, nor which might *make* them a spirit. Both brothers drank deeply, and Gartrelle fell dead.

Godfrey Barnsley survived, but didn't truly win. It turned out that Chessie had been in love with Gartrelle, the brother who died.

This tradition of bloodshed between brothers unfortunately ran in the family. Years later, Godfrey Barnsley's great-grandson, Preston Saylor, feared that his sibling Harry was conspiring to have him committed to a mental asylum. Preston shot his brother, who collapsed into the arms of his mother and died.

12 West Oglethorpe

Many houses in Savannah have a reputation for being haunted. In fact, it has been said that having a ghost or two in an old structure downtown has become something of a status symbol. In many interviews with locals, one house was consistently mentioned as being inhabited with otherworldly presences: the crumbling edifice of 12 West Oglethorpe. The structure has been vacant for many years—its most continuous use was as a Fraternal Lodge Meeting Hall. What is it about this vacant house that inspires such a feeling of dread?

One Savannahian revealed to me that she used to run past the house as a little girl. "My sister and I were terrified of that house, and we were convinced it was haunted. This was long before it was vacant. Years later I read *To Kill a Mockingbird*, and I suddenly realized that we treated 12 West Oglethorpe exactly like the children in the book treated Boo Radley's house. We came up with all sorts of crazy stories of who haunted it and why."

Noted Savannah author Murray Silver has taken several photos of the exterior of the house, and in those photos some surprising things appear. In several shots, an image that can be interpreted as a face appears faintly in one of the windows, although the house was deserted at the time the photographs were taken.

Indeed, the local ghost tours seem fascinated by the house, as well. One story told about the house is that a doctor lived there, and in his attempts to battle Yellow Fever, he somehow transferred the disease to his children, who succumbed to the dreaded disease. The aforementioned doctor now supposedly haunts the house, grieving for his lost children. This tale is unlikely for a number of reasons: Yellow Fever was spread by mosquitoes, and was not communicable from person to person. Also, an exhaustive search of the records reveals that no doctor ever lived in the house. The closest bit of truth to anyone remotely medical living in the area was a dentist (Dr. Samuel White)—and he lived next door. This story is likely imported from Charleston, because the tale bears a striking resemblance to an epitaph (in a graveyard right off of Church St.) written about three young brothers in the Savage family who all died within days of each other—and their father was indeed a doctor battling the disease. Another story told is that a woman hanged herself after losing her baby. This story is also unsubstantiated as of the time of this writing.

Another fact that has thus far eluded this researcher is the actual date the building was erected. Conflicting records make this difficult to ascertain. According to an online search via tax records, the structure dates from 1900. An initial look at the Georgia Historical archives reveals this to be accurate—at least in theory. The records show that there was a new improvement by Beirne Gordon (partners with William Washington Gordon, Juliette Gordon Low's father, in a shipping company) in 1898. The listing is for a two story brick house built on the lot in question. But there are several indicators that suggest that this was merely an improvement to an existing property. A little known fact is that Nellie Gordon never got along with her husband's mother, Sarah. Willie and Nellie Gordon actually moved from the Gordon mansion (currently known as the Birthplace) to a house built at 12 West Oglethorpe— a short distance away from the Birthplace— after the Civil War, and it appears that they lived there until Sarah passed away in the 1880's. So records indicate that the property on which 12 West Oglethorpe currently sits was already in the Gordon name as early as the end of the 1860's, meaning that Willie and Nellie Gordon, along with Juliette Gordon Low and the rest of the Gordon clan lived at a structure that at least was *located* at 12 West Oglethorpe Avenue, for at least fifteen years and perhaps as many as twenty.

The house was sold in 1908 to the Elk's Lodge. It remained in their hands for many years before becoming a school. The structure finally became vacant in the late 1980's.

But strange stories persist regarding 12 West Oglethorpe. The neighbors on the lower floor of the apartment house right next door report hearing pots and pans banging, and the sounds of cooking taking place from inside the darkened edifice. And the upstairs neighbor in the same building has reported seeing an old man through an adjacent window. From his bathroom sink he can see into the structure, and has both seen and heard an elderly man crying—and when he asked the realtor for the property about the identity of the person in the obviously abandoned site, the real estate agent gave him a strange look and explained that the window he was asking about *had no floor underneath to support anyone.* He had seen someone apparently standing on thin air. The neighbor dealt with this in a uniquely Savannah way: he bought drapes for the kitchen window so he wouldn't see the man who wasn't there anymore.

Just what is the fascination with this vacant building in the heart of downtown? Perhaps the future holds the key to past events still unfolding. The rest of the story remains to be written, but if history is any indicator, we have not heard the last about 12 West Oglethorpe.

Wrong Passenger, Wright Square?

Till you know about the living, how are you to know about the dead?

—Confucius

In yet another strange happening experienced by local historian Rebecca Clark, there was an incident where she picked up an unwanted spectral hitchhiker one night right off of Wright Square. "I was returning to my car one evening," she explained, "And as soon as I reached it I knew something bizarre was happening. When I opened my car door, I felt a rush of icy cold air gush out, even though it was a steamy Savannah summer night and the car had been sitting for several hours."

As soon as she leaned into the car she could feel something was seriously amiss. "I felt a presence so strong, I literally looked behind the front seat to see if someone was crouching there, out of view. Of course, there was no one there—at least not physically there, anyway. I started the engine and began to drive, all the while expecting to see someone sitting in my back seat in the rear view mirror. I actually stopped at a red light and got out of my car for a moment. Now, this was not the best neighborhood, but I actually felt safer on the street than in my front seat of my car! I got back in when the light changed and made my way back home, but I never lost that feeling of being watched, and it felt unfriendly.

"Once I pulled into my driveway, I got out of that car as quick as I could, and locked up and went to bed. My golden retriever Bella ran to me on the bed, and after that strange experience I was glad to have the company. But even Bella was acting odd—she hid under the covers, which is totally unlike her. And that's when it happened:

"Down the hall in the study, every single electrical device went haywire. The television, the VCR, the stereo, the computer—everything turned on by itself and began to blare. I was so frightened. I've had numerous experiences with ghosts and whatnot, but nothing like this. All I could do was close the bedroom door. I wasn't going in there, and one look at Bella cowering under the covers told me she wasn't going in there, either. Whatever or whoever that strange spirit was, they had not only followed me home, they were now in my office study!

"The next morning, I woke up and looked in the office, and nothing was amiss. All of the electrical devices were in the 'off' position, and it was like the whole thing never happened. Even Bella seemed fine.

"Two or three days later, I had to go back downtown. As soon as I opened my car door, I figured out where the entity was: they were waiting in the car! I felt that same icy blast of air from my car even though it was a hot day as soon as the door swung open. The whole ride downtown, I tried to talk to the spirit. Anyone seeing me talking to no one would just figure I was singing along with the radio, I guess. But I basically told whoever it was that I was going back downtown, and they could just get out whenever they wanted.

"As soon as I got near Wright Square, I felt them leave, and that was the last experience I had with them."

If the preceding story, told by a historian, is true (giving it even more credibility is that it bears a striking resemblance to a similar story involving the Olde Pink House's talented pianist, Gail Thurmond, also detailed in this volume), then we must consider the fact that while we may sometimes take ghost tours, the reverse can also occur. Sometimes Savannahians can act as unwitting chauffeurs for the departed.

Old Cemeteries

Good friends, for Jesus' sake forbear

To dig the dust enclosed here

Blest be the man that spares these stones

And curst be he that moves my bones

-William Shakespeare's epitaph

Savannah, if the pun can be forgiven, has a grave problem. The amount of renovation taking place in Georgia's First City is turning up the obvious remnants of her close ties with a tragic past: graves in odd locations. Finding bodies while digging in Savannah is extremely common, as this and other chapters will explore (see chapters entitled "Foley House," "Marshall House," and "Colonial Cemetery" for more on the discovery of makeshift or previously unknown graves).

The most obvious question is: *why would this occur?* There is no easy answer, but perhaps this author can shed some light on a few of the reasons Savannahians might engage in either improper burials, or conversely, improper burial *removal.* Attitudes over the years have changed drastically over how a deceased individual's corpse is treated. In this writer's opinion, this modern society in which we live today has a virtual phobia regarding death. The sick are removed to hospitals or nursing home facilities, and there is a brief viewing of the cadaver (which has been sanitized and only after the body has had makeup applied) before burial.

However, in the past, death was much more commonplace—think of the high infant mortality rates, improper or archaic medical care (which often consisted of trial-and-error), and the fact that many women died during childbirth. Couple that with the knowledge that people who were near death were rarely taken out of the family dwelling, seeing as how there were few hospitals or geriatric care facilities. Most deaths occurred at home, and the funerals were held there, as well. The front doors of houses served double-duty, as once they were removed and placed in the parlor, they became so-called 'cooling boards', a platform used to display the deceased loved one. If the family was Irish, there would be a party called a 'wake', essentially a combination of mourning the loss and celebrating the life of the departed individual all at once. (The old joke—Q: What is the difference between an Irish wake and an Irish wedding? A: One less drunk.) To be a resident of any city during that time period, regardless of station in life, was to be well-acquainted with the spectre of death.

Another contributing factor to the strange habit of burying the dead in unusual places was the scarcity of unused plots in approved cemeteries, and the subsequent abandonment of one burial ground for another. This began very early in this city's history. Colonial Park Cemetery is widely regarded as the oldest cemetery in Georgia, but it bears that honor with an asterisk. Colonial Park Cemetery is the oldest still in existence, but not the first. The site of the very first cemetery in Georgia was actually located on the southwest corner of present day Wright Square. It was only in use during the first 17 years of the city's existence. There was also a Jewish burial ground located towards the south of the original cemetery which is still there, located in the median of Oglethorpe Avenue. At last count, at least sixteen bodies are still interred there, nestled between east- and westbound lanes of one of Savannah's main downtown thoroughfares.

The city opened a new cemetery a few blocks east to ease overcrowding, which came to be known as Colonial Park Cemetery, in 1750. There is only a brass plaque flanking Wright Square on York Street to commemorate the Protestant graves located in this first burial ground, which incidentally are still there. The graves were not moved into the new cemetery, and the city allowed the plot of land to be developed. As easy as this would be to ascribe to the rampant laziness present in early Savannah, actually the townsfolk had a much more practical reason for not moving the bodies into the new cemetery: they feared disease. Many of the dead had succumbed to Yellow Fever, a dreaded killer, as well as many other types of disease that the early Savannahians feared would still be communicable.

Any type of construction that takes place in that location that involves digging has to be done very carefully because of all the bodies still located under the buildings, back lane (alley) and street.

Some road crews and utility companies have been accompanied by an archaeologist, and they usually turn up a few of Georgia's earliest inhabitants when they do any sort of maintenance. A man working for Georgia Power who asked not to be identified relayed a grisly tale about laying some cable in that area using a machine that burrows sideways through the ground. He said, "A human body makes a sound unlike any other when that machine bores through it. We are supposed to keep a log of when we hear that sound. When we laid a cable in the alley running behind that area, I was busy all day writing down the fact that we kept hitting body... after body... after body." He then described the sound, likening it to a wooden spoon caught in a garbage disposal.

To put into perspective how many bodies are buried here, we had 114 original settlers that accompanied James Edward Oglethorpe in 1733. One year later, half of them were dead. And that's just the passengers on one ship, and one year out of 17. There are hundreds, and perhaps thousands, of bodies here. But perhaps there are a few less, thanks to Georgia Power.

But this is not an isolated case. A Savannah Morning News article from 1878 reveals that a man digging a ditch on the far western edge of Bryan St. struck something with his spade. Examination proved it to be a small coffin-like box, and inside it contained the body of an infant.

According to a December 14th, 1927 Savannah Morning News article, a body was unearthed by a crew laying storm drains on Gordon Lane, which is the alley to the south of Gordon Street. The crew found a crumbling coffin with a human skeleton inside, which they unearthed in full view of children out on recess from the Massie School, located just north on Calhoun Square. According to the article, the children, rather than being sickened or afraid, were highly excited that there were people buried so close to their school.

Further examination revealed several skeletons, including one which had been decapitated (presumably by the road crew), pine boxes, and a few crumbling headstones. Research shows that this is the location of an old slave burial ground, which is shown on an 1818 map of the city, titled clearly 'Negro Burial Ground'. During that time period, the area was the South Common, before any houses and certainly before any *schools* were built on the location. Supposedly the bodies were moved in 1855 to the African-American section of Laurel Grove Cemetery (South) to make way for city expansion—but apparently more than a few bodies were missed, perhaps on purpose. There was a fee being charged by the city to remove bodies from the old burial ground, and more than a few families either could not afford the charge, or authorities were unable to locate next-of-kin.

How many burials remain from this nearly forgotten cemetery? Without a significant and expensive archaeological dig to find out, the question will remain unanswered, but there are apparently quite a few. As late as June of 2004, human remains were found by a utility crew in this location, this time digging in *front* of the school. This was reported in the Savannah Morning News, with an accompanying picture of a Savannah-Chatham Metro police officer holding aloft a skull at the dig site.

Yet another recent incident involving the police in Savannah was during the 2004 construction of the Mansion on Forsyth, a sprawling luxury hotel on the eastern side of Forsyth Park. As the crew dug the foundation, they began to encounter bodies in coffins, or occasionally human remains *sans* casket. Repeatedly, the police (and county coroner) would be called and the construction would be delayed. The encountering of human remains eventually became so commonplace that the law enforcement instructed the crew to simply move the coffins or remains to one side and continue digging. The authorities would then come by and collect them when there were several coffins, thus saving the police the trouble of numerous trips.

Even stranger than the reaction of the police and coroner was the fact that no one seems to know why these bodies are turning up in that location. No evidence has surfaced of the area ever being an approved area for burials or cemetery plot. A likely scenario involves the close proximity of the old Candler Hospital, located just north along Forsyth Park. It is entirely possible that victims of Yellow Fever were buried in secret (and illegally!) by the hospital staff. If this theory is correct, this was probably to avert causing a panic within the populace if the true far-reaching impact of the disease became common knowledge.

This story proves once again that the wheels of bureaucracy turn slowly in Savannah, even when those aforementioned wheels are responding to the finding of human remains. After all, this is not an unusual occurrence.

Savannah is truly a city built on the dead.

Alice Riley

Many storytellers tell a tale about Alice Riley, the first person executed in Georgia, in 1735. Some claim that she practiced witchcraft, and was hanged because she was a murderess and practiced black magic. A common claim is that she cursed the city from the gallows in Wright Square, and this reason is given as to why no Spanish Moss will grow in the trees near where she was hanged. The likely source of these stories of witchcraft is probably a case of mistaken identity, confusing Savannah's Alice Riley with Charleston's Lavinia Fisher, who was hanged in 1820 (Fisher did indeed have some colorful things to say from the scaffold, reputedly saying, "If you have a message for the Devil, give it to me, for I am about to meet him!"). The historical record shows that the witchcraft angle for Riley and the curse are fiction, but Alice Riley's tale is surprising in its own right.

✎The Murder✎

Alice Riley was one of roughly forty Irish servants who landed in Savannah in December of 1733. James Edward Oglethorpe charitably bought their indentures for five pounds apiece, and the magistrates of Savannah placed Alice and a fellow named Richard White into the household of William Wise. Wise was an unsavory character, already having tried unsuccessfully to pass off a common London prostitute as his daughter in hopes of bringing her to Georgia. Wise had property out on Hutchinson Island, located across the Savannah River from present-day River Street. He tended the Trustee's cattle, but was unable to perform his duties because of illness. Presumably, Riley and White were placed with Wise to help care for the livestock, but Wise had other ideas.

William Wise made it a habit to call for his servants to bathe and groom him. He would lie with his head positioned off the bed so White could comb his long hair, while Riley bathed him. In March of

1734, the two Irish immigrants murdered him together, both by twisting Wise's neckerchief and slipping his head into the bucket of water.

The two were caught and sentenced to hang on the gallows, but Alice was found to be pregnant. The child is credited to White, but considering Wise's previous actions with the streetwalker one must at least raise the possibility of the child belonging to the lecherous master.

The death sentence was delayed until the child was born, but on January 19th, 1735, Alice Riley was hung by the neck until dead for the crime of murder. White was hanged the following day. Both Riley and White steadfastly maintained their innocence to the end. No evidence exists of Riley's involvement in witchcraft, or of her cursing anyone or anything from the scaffold. Nonetheless, the hanging of Alice Riley and Richard White spawned a number of firsts: first murder in the colony of Georgia, and first execution in Georgia, both of a man and a woman.

Alice Riley's child did not survive, bringing the death toll for the whole sorry affair to four.

✥Strange Savannah✥

As a postscript, one wonders why, out of the many stories available to tour guides, not one speaks of the many, many other candidates for folklore in Savannah? There is no shortage of stories full of the bizarre and grotesque. Take for example Rebecca Cheeswright. If ever there were a candidate for folklore, it is Rebecca, who was sentenced in 1735 to sixty lashes in the town square. Her crime? She took a knife and sliced a helpless infant down the back.

And let's not forget Jesse McKethan, a.k.a. the Butcher Murderer, who in 1945 choked his best friend Luther lifeless and then dismembered the corpse with a hatchet, leaving a trail of body parts for the police to follow. Their quarrel allegedly stemmed from Jesse's jealousy for Luther's affections. A wonderful version of the 'Butcher Murderer' story is recounted in Murray Silver's great book, *Behind the Moss Curtain*.

There was a woman in 1808 who so neglected her stepchildren, James and William Bayley, that they died of both exposure and malnutrition from eating dirt, respectively.

Captain John Darthigue shot himself in the head, using not one but *two* pistols, fired simultaneously. Darthigue's overkill ironically turned into a case of underkill, because he survived both gunshots for nearly ten agonizing days before finally succumbing to his wounds.

In 1909, a triple murder occurred at a house at the corner of Montgomery and Perry Streets. Three women were found, two dead and one mortally wounded. The trio had been assaulted with an axe, and possibly a hammer.

And as recently as 2003, the girl crowned Miss Savannah was charged with shooting and killing her boyfriend over a dispute regarding his fidelity. The most surprising aspect of the case is that her crown was not removed—she was allowed to finish out her term as Miss Savannah.

Savannah truly is a place that celebrates the bizarre. The strange case of Alice Riley is just one of a myriad of strange and unusual happenings that make Savannah a unique and colorful city.

Juliette Gordon Low's Birthplace

Many houses in Savannah have a great amount of history, but perhaps none so much as the imposing mansion located at the corner of Bull St. and Oglethorpe Avenue, the birthplace of Juliette Gordon Low. Many Savannah residents simply call it The Birthplace instead of its proper title, the Wayne-Gordon House. The Regency-style house, completed in 1821, is thought to be a William Jay design, the same architect as the Owens-Thomas House. However, it is possible that the structure was built by a protégé of Jay's, perhaps the same unknown architect who designed the old City Hotel.

Juliette Gordon Low founded the Girl Guides, which later became the Girl Scouts. The house today is used as the National Center of Girl Scouts, and is visited by approximately eighty thousand Girl

Scouts every year. But beyond the story of Juliette, one of the most liberated women of the past 150 years, we find the tender love story of her parents.

Juliette's father, William Washington Gordon II, was also born in the house, and it is here that he brought his new bride, Nellie Kinzie, in 1858. It is one of the family's favorite stories that Willie fell in love with Nellie in 1853, when she slid down the main staircase of the Yale Library at New Haven and crushed his brand new hat. She maintained that high-spirited habit of sliding down banisters all her life.

☙Clashing Feminine Personalities☙

When Nellie moved in, it meant the house then had two strong personalities: she and the lady of the house: Willie's mother, Sarah Gordon. The two did not always see eye to eye. Nellie was upset, a letter to her mother reveals, that Sarah required her son Willie to give half of his paycheck to her.

Three children were born to Willie and Nellie before the country went to war. In what Nellie called 'The Confederate War', Willie served the Confederacy in the Georgia Hussars, and was wounded in the Battle of Atlanta. Nellie never lost that spark that had attracted Willie: her brother and uncle were fighting for the Union, and so a woman remarked to her, "I hope that the first shot fired will kill (your brother) dead." Nellie later ran into the same woman, and said, "I hear that your brother has been shot in the back. Mine is doing quite well, thank you." So deep and abiding was her love for Willie that Nellie found the need to track him down not once, but twice—once enlisting the aid of Confederate General Robert E. Lee, and the other with the help of Union General William T. Sherman.

When General Sherman occupied Savannah, he and his officers came to pay their respects to Eleanor Kinzie Gordon. Accompanying Sherman was Brigadier General O. O. Howard, who was notable because he had lost an arm during the Battle of Seven Pines. Eleanor's daughter, Daisy (whom we know today as Juliette Gordon Low, founder of the Girl Scouts) noticed that Howard was missing an arm. She, with the charming tactlessness of a child, asked how he lost his arm. Howard replied that a Confederate soldier had *shot* his arm off.

Daisy then wondered aloud, "I wonder if my Papa didn't do it? He has shot lots of Yankees!" No one laughed harder than William T. Sherman.

After the war, Willie and Nellie were reunited, and three more children were born in the Gordon household.

When Nellie visited her daughter Juliette in England, Rudyard Kipling put her in a story as "a little old lady with snapping black eyes, who used very bad language." Nellie thanked him for the honor.

When Willie passed away in 1912, Nellie was devastated. She wrote a cousin: "My strict observance of the 5th Commandment has resulted in my 'living long in the land'... unless it is because the Lord doesn't want me, and the Devil doesn't either. At any rate, here I remain, very much against my will, for there is nothing I so sincerely desire in this world as to get out of it."

Nellie was ill in the fall of 1916, and a doctor ordered her confined to her to bed on the third floor. She was to avoid stairs at all costs. The family met to discuss the dividing up of the estate, but did so in secret on the second floor as to not upset Nellie. Suddenly Nellie appeared in the doorway, and admonished them all for treating her as if she was already in the grave. When the family began to chastise her for disobeying the doctor, Nellie smiled and told them that she hadn't—she had given her word that she couldn't use the stairs, so she slid down the banister!

She passed away in 1917, but before she did, she was adamant about no one 'wearing mourning'. She would be with Willie again in the afterlife, so everyone should celebrate.

Nellie died in her bedroom on Washington's Birthday, February 22, 1917. Her daughter-in-law Margaret reported that she was surprised to see her father-in-law, who had died five years ago, coming out of Nellie's bedroom. He was wearing his grey officer's uniform, and his face was one of extreme joy. He walked down the front stairs and out of sight. It was then that another family member walked out of the same doorway to Nellie's bedroom and told her that Nellie had just passed away. Margaret told of seeing Willie Gordon, but her claims were dismissed... that is, until they walked to the foyer. The old family butler was standing at the foot of the stairs, tears streaming down his cheeks. Before they could speak, he told them that he had just seen Willie in his General's uniform, walking down the stairs, looking ever so happy. The man went on to say that the General must have come back to fetch Nellie himself.

Her children said that when Nellie died, her face took on the radiance of a bride.

∾Place of History, Place of Hauntings∾

The house museum today has been restored to reflect the 1880's. Among the collection of art and antiques is artwork created by Daisy herself. Members of the museum staff claim that Willie and Nellie are still happy and together in the house. The piano in the south parlor is heard to play from time to time—which is amazing considering that it has been broken since the 1940's. Both Nellie and her mother-in-law, Sarah Gordon, were accomplished musicians.

The Juliette Gordon Low Birthplace was featured on the Travel Channel program 'America's Most Haunted Places- Savannah'. In the segment, several people gave firsthand accounts of seeing strange sights at the house. Tour guides claim that the presence of Sarah, and not Willie or Nellie, is the foremost spectre in the house. It stands to reason that a woman so dominant in life would also be somewhat prominent in the household even after her passing. In the upstairs office, the adding machine would be found by a senior staff member in the mornings to have jumbles of numbers on the paper and it would be scrolling out of the machine. Exasperated, she finally unplugged the device before leaving for the night. When she returned in the morning, the machine was once again found to be used—with the paper scrolled out onto the floor, but the power cord was still disconnected from the wall. Later, she actually saw the machine while it was tabulating on its own, with the cord unplugged from the wall and no fingers actually pressing the keys.

∾Sarah's Overbearing Presence∾

Guides also report that as soon as the elevator was installed, Sarah began to make appearances from time to time. A strange instance in the elevator illustrates Sarah's presence in the house. A special code must be entered in order to access the third floor, but on Missy Brandt's first day working at the Birthplace, it took her unerringly to the third floor, which opens next to Sarah's old room, without her touching any buttons. Sarah is also reported to be seen at times, wearing a dark brown dress, in various rooms of the old house.

Sometimes, working at such a haunted location means you have to take things in stride. A guide in the house smiled broadly when I asked her about Sarah's ghost. "Well, I had a couple of Girl Scouts come back from the bathroom and comment that it was 'pretty neat' that we had installed those motion-activated sinks in the bathroom, because the water turned on as soon as the Scouts got near them— and it was surprising that the water was so hot. I'd say it's surprising: we don't have motion-activated sinks, and the water isn't hot in the bathroom! But I pretended as if nothing was amiss because I didn't want to create a stampede of girls towards the bathroom."

One night, a special evening tour was to take place. The guides arrived to open the Birthplace and found the interior lights blazing, when they had been shut off earlier that day. On another occasion, a ghost tour guide telling the story outside reported seeing something strange through one of the windows. A woman in period costume was seen by the guide and the entire walking tour through one of the southern parlors, carrying a candle. Inquiries the next day at the Birthplace revealed that no events had taken place the previous night.

A tour guide named Diane, walking up the stairs to the third floor carrying a heavy package, suddenly lost her footing and was about to take a fall that possibly could have been fatal. She felt a firm hand plant itself squarely in her back and push her back to her feet. She turned around to thank whoever had possibly saved her life—and found no one on the stairs behind her.

The ghosts in this house apparently lend a helping hand from time to time.

The Juliette Gordon Low Birthplace is open to the public. The hours of operation are:

10:00 a.m.-4:00 p.m. on Mon., Tues., Thu., Fri., and Saturday; 12:30 p.m.-4:30 p.m. on Sunday.
Closed on Wednesdays

Colonial Park Cemetery

"Now! I want to die now!"

—The final words of Daniel Wilson, age eight
as recorded on his tombstone in Colonial Park Cemetery

Tour guide Karl Kessler followed closely by an intense orb.

Colonial Park Cemetery is the oldest cemetery in Savannah. By very definition it chronicles the tragic events which have befallen Georgia's First City: interred here are the victims of fire, disease, murder and war. Colonial Park has another reputation other than a cross-section of Savannah's hardships... the whispers that perhaps those victims of tragedy rest uneasy. There have also been bizarre findings within the cemetery grounds which necessitate the City locking the iron gates every night.

Opened in 1750, it was used as Savannah's primary burial ground for 103 years. Included among the noteworthy burials here are Revolutionary War heroes such as Button Gwinnett, a signer of the Declaration of Independence; Generals Lachlan McIntosh and Samuel Elbert; Archibald Bulloch, 1st President of Georgia, and Maj. William Leigh Pierce. But Colonial Park Cemetery is not simply a collection of war heroes. It is filled with ordinary people whose weathered headstones tell much about their struggles and triumphs. Standing in Colonial Park Cemetery, we are surrounded by people from all walks of life; the merchants, carpenters, captains, doctors, wives, husbands, and children. This is a place of mass graves. We have duelists and suicides buried alongside the statesmen and captains of industry. All of these people have stories to tell; here is a brief offering:

There are about 600 burial markers, but over 11,000 bodies interred here. The oldest gravestone still remaining is that of William Bower Williamson, who died in 1762. It is just a fragment, having been damaged throughout the years.

Scattered throughout the cemetery are brick vaults. These are family vaults. At first glance they appear to be above- ground burials, but this is not the case. A sealed-over archway on one side marks the former entrance, and a series of steps, long- since filled in with earth, once led down into the vaults. Once inside, you would find a row of three shelves on either side, which contained either a coffin, or in some cases, a shrouded corpse. In the center of the vault floor would be placed a large urn. When the vault became crowded and the shelves were full, the older burials would be placed inside the urn to save room. As time passed, more bones would be added to the urn as more space was needed—and this also reinforced the idea of the family being together, in this case literally, in death.

Odrey Miller, who died in a duel in 1831, has an intriguing gravestone: his friends made sure that the man who shot Odrey Miller was named on his tombstone for posterity. The killer apparently took exception to being recorded in stone as a murderer. Presumably under cover of darkness, he crept into the cemetery and chiseled his name off of Odrey Miller's slab.

Samuel Elbert attained the rank of Brigadier General in the Continental Army. He also served as Governor of Georgia, a Trustee of Chatham Academy, and Sheriff of Chatham County. When he passed away, he was buried originally at his plantation, called Rae's Hall. The burial ground at Rae's Hall was a large Indian mound, known as 'the 'Mount', located about 5 miles upriver, that had previously been a burial ground for the Indians that predated the Yamacraw in the area. There he and the remains of his wife remained in the old Indian burial mound until 1915, when a group of children from prominent Savannah families decided to hunt for arrowheads and artifacts in the mound. Instead they found some bones, which were actually two skeletons, along with coffin handles, and nails. The boys were thrilled with their discovery, and they dug up the bones and took them home. But the excitement of their find was quickly dulled when an article in the newspaper a few days later announced that vandals had desecrated the grave of Samuel Elbert, Revolutionary War hero. One of the boys, in a panic, threw some of the bones away. The remaining bones were eventually taken to the Georgia Historical Society, and turned in to a librarian there, where they remained in a drawer for several years. Finally in 1924, amid great ceremony, the bones were placed in Colonial Park Cemetery. It is still not known whether the bones actually belonged to Elbert, his wife, or perhaps another family member. And what of the bones discarded? It is entirely possible that *these* bones were the remains of Samuel Elbert. The Revolutionary War hero and politician could be buried in a less- than- honorable location: the city dump.

Susannah Gray's stone informs us that she "departed this life by the will of God, being killed by lightning on the 26th, July 1812." Her correct age is 21 years, not the 121 years, 1124 days that is listed on her stone. This alteration is the handiwork of the Union troops in Sherman's army, who camped in the cemetery in 1864. Another changed stone is Josiah Muir, whose altered inscription reads that he died at the age of eleven, and was survived by his wife Mary, age seventeen, and his son Lewis, aged twelve. Among many others that the Union troops changed are Captain Jonathan Cooper, aged 1700 years, and Phillip D. Woolhopter, aged 1491.

There are thought to be two more rows of graves out beyond the fence bordering Abercorn St. When the City put in the sidewalk in 1896, the headstones were removed and the bodies left in place. Several of these bodies were discovered in 1967 when roadwork was done on Abercorn. The bodies were moved into the cemetery and marked with a plain concrete marker.

The epitaph on the John Struthers, Esq., marker was written by his brother, Robert. Upon the death of John, Robert inherited the

Glasgow Brewery—so not only is there a glowing account of John's life on the gravestone, there is also an advertisement for the brewery.

Lining the wall are headstones that were displaced and vandalized throughout the years, including damage done by both the British and Union troops when they occupied the city.

The year 1820 was one of devastation. Savannah was struck with a Great Fire, burning much of downtown. She was then struck a second time—not with fire, but with a terrible fever. An epidemic of Yellow Fever killed a tenth of the population, totaling nearly seven hundred people. Symptoms included black bloody vomit, a jaundiced color, hemorrhages from the nose, gums, and bowels, and a fever-induced descent into delirium. Dr. James J. Waring tried to combat the disease. He also tried to figure out what the cause was, so he kept a careful log of temperatures, locations that the plague seemed prevalent and attempted cures he administered. One remedy he tried was giving a large dose of turpentine for the victim to drink. Another 'remedy' used since Colonial days was to drink water mixed with tar.

It would be eighty years before the carrier of yellow fever was known: the mosquito.

A Sickening Discovery

In 1999 and early 2000, the cemetery was also the site of either a voodoo ceremony, or an especially cruel and morbid practical joke. In late 1999, a dog with its throat slashed was found in the cemetery. It was a terrible thing to have happen, but especially downtown in a cemetery nestled between the police barracks and the fire house. But the awful findings were just beginning: in April of that following year, local historian and cemetery enthusiast Elizabeth Piechocinski was walking her dog, Cedric, next to Colonial Park when she spotted something which didn't belong on one of the burial slabs. Closer investigation revealed a dead goat. The goat's mouth and feet had been bound, the throat slashed, and the heart had been cut out. Found nearby was the goat's heart in foil, a coconut, and a burned candle. Whether this was a voodoo ceremony, some sort of Satanic ritual or a horrible and tasteless joke has never been determined.

Orbs surrounding eagle atop entrance to Colonial Park Cemetery.

Headstones against the East wall of Colonial Park Cemetery.

The City of Savannah, perhaps embarrassed by the close proximity of the police barracks to the scene of the desecration, now locks the gates of Colonial Park every evening at 8 p.m.

A Personal Sighting?

One bizarre happening in Colonial Park with possible supernatural ties was experienced by this author. In late November, 2001, I was beginning my second ghost tour, which began at 9 o'clock. I was standing at the beautiful granite arched entrance and had just begun my introduction to the crowd—essentially telling them who I was and what they could expect on the tour. The temperature had dropped precipitously all throughout the evening, and the crowd began to pull in closer to me, perhaps in an effort to keep warm. Suddenly, I noticed that several people in the group were staring at something over my shoulder with expressions ranging from amazement to out-and-out fear. After being distracted by this for a few minutes and attempting to keep going regardless, I finally stopped talking and turned around. What I saw in the cemetery made my blood run even colder: about twenty yards away, near the marker for Edward Malbone, painter of miniatures, there was a strange mist.

This was a vapor unlike any I had ever seen. It appeared to be tendrils of mist, swirling up out of the ground, and it only rose from four or five spots all densely packed together. These tendrils were rising up in columns, swirling even though there was no breeze at all. No where else in the cemetery was there even fog, let alone strange mist, except in this one isolated location. These columns rose about five and a half feet off of the ground—it was pointed out to me later by one of the witnesses that these phenomena were roughly as tall as a human, which I admit never occurred to me at the time. My entire tour group and I watched this unbelievable sight for a full three minutes until the strange vaporous forms gradually dissipated. I turned back to the group, who were full of questions about what they had just seen. One person actually accused me of somehow staging the incident!

Brittney's Ancestor Hunt

Another strange happening which could be deemed by some as paranormal would be Brittney Hall's experience in Colonial Park Cemetery. Brittney moved to Savannah six years ago, and in a conversation with her family she learned that she has ancestors buried in Colonial Park. Brittney decided one day while walking her dog to look for the name on the tombstone. It was a daunting task, with over six hundred burial markers in the burial ground. Not having any idea where the stone was located, or if it even survived, she simply entered the cemetery and began to walk.

Brittney walked unerringly to the far east wall and found the stone in a matter of minutes. "I had never even been inside that cemetery before, but somehow I knew just where to look," she said.

Was this simply coincidence? Or was it instead a case of collective memory, of Brittney somehow 'remembering' where a dead relative was buried, even though she had never walked through the cemetery before? One can never tell in Savannah.

Colonial Park Cemetery is open to the public from 8 a.m.- 8 p.m. daily. Leaving promptly at 8 p.m. is recommended—it is rather easy for the caretaker of the cemetery to inadvertently lock you inside.

Much of the history quoted in this story came from Elizabeth Piechocinski's wonderful book, "The Old Burying Ground: Colonial Park Cemetery." This author enthusiastically recommends her book to anyone interested in learning more about Colonial Park.

Conrad Aiken

Conrad Aiken was one of Savannah's most famous literary figures, along with Flannery O'Connor and Joel Chandler Harris. Aiken was a celebrated and decorated 20th century poet and author. But his life was marked with both tragedy as well as triumph.

Born in 1889, Conrad grew up in a row of houses called Marshall Row located across from Colonial Park Cemetery. He recalled later in life that he and his friends played amongst the tombstones, and in his autobiography entitled *Ushant, An Essay* published in 1952, he referred to it as "that jungle graveyard." He recalled that "one could pry loose the bricks of the ancient vaults and crawl down into the warm dust to find broken boards and an old brown bone or two." An excerpt from his poem, *The Coming Forth by Day of Osiris Jones*, mentions the cemetery and surrounding environs thusly:

> *The house in Broad Street, red brick, with nine rooms*
> *the weedgrown graveyard with its row of tombs*
> *the jail from which imprisoned faces grinned*
> *at stiff palmettos flashing in the wind*
>
> *the engine-house, with engines and a tank*
> *in which young alligators swam and stank,*
> *the bell-tower, of red iron, where the bell*
> *gonged of the fires in a tone from hell.*

His father William, a doctor, began to exhibit signs of what Conrad later described as the family petit mal of mental instability. He believed that his wife was trying to have him committed to an asylum, and surrounded himself with paranoid delusions. An associate asked William how he was doing, and he responded, "For an answer to that question I shall have to refer you to my lawyer."

His father's instability increased, and he tried on several occasions to take his own life. In one instance he turned the gas on in the apartment, informing his wife that they "would now see who would emerge from the apartment alive," according to the Savannah Morning News' account of the Aiken tragedy.

Aiken quarreled with his wife during the last week of February, 1901. Eleven-year-old Conrad, who was home at the time, heard a silence and then his father's voice counting to three. Then he heard a pistol shot. He heard his father count again, and then another pistol shot sounded, and he heard what sounded like a body hitting the floor. Conrad rushed to the nearby police station and told the desk sergeant that "Papa has just shot Mama and then himself."

Conrad was sent north to Massachusetts to live with relatives. He went on to write numerous poems and authored several novels. During the First World War, Aiken claimed that he was in an 'essential industry' because of being a poet, and was granted an exemption for that reason. Aiken, during his illustrious career, held the poetry chair at the library of Congress from 1950-57 and was awarded the National Medal for Literature in 1969.

☞The Great Circle☜

Aiken moved back to Savannah in 1962, and bought the house right next door to his childhood home. At first glance, to live next door to where his father shot his mother and then himself would appear morbid, but Aiken claimed that he had happy memories of the area. Also, the idea of ending up where one began would appeal to Conrad. It had both a literal and figurative meaning for him: he had even written a novel about the subject ('Great Circle', 1933). This cyclical idea is strengthened by the fact that Conrad lived his first eleven years in Savannah, and his last eleven years, as well: matching bookends to his life in matching houses on the same street. He died in 1973.

Aiken did visit his parents before his death, out in Bonaventure Cemetery on the far eastern side of the city. They were interred in one of the most beautiful sections of the cemetery, close to Johnny Mercer's grave and within sight of the river. While he was there, he saw a ship passing in the Wilmington River with the name 'Cosmos Mariner'. It struck a lyrical chord with Conrad, so he checked the Shipping News for more information. The ship named Cosmos Mariner had a destination listed as 'Unknown'. This turn of phrase delighted Conrad, and he felt a kinship with the vessel.

Conrad specified that when he died, he wanted to be buried near his parents, but rather than a statue or large burial vault, he wanted a bench. It is a Savannah tradition to sit on Aiken's grave and toast him with either a martini or a mint julep. The inscription on the bench says:

Conrad Aiken

Cosmos Mariner

Destination Unknown

Duelling in Savannah

Set honor in one eye and death i' th' other,

And I will look on both indifferently;

For let the gods so speed me as I love

The name of honor more than I fear death.

-William Shakespeare
Julius Caesar

Early Savannah had a tradition which traced back to the colony's English roots: the practice of duelling. The practice was sometimes referred to as 'pistols for two, coffin for one.' The convention of one man facing down an adversary continued until after the War Between the States. The rules of the engagement, called the Code Duello, were lengthy and placed limits on the scope of the confrontation.

There were rules for when a duel was appropriate, rules of conduct, and rules for when the challenge had been satisfied. Although interpretations varied, there was an accepted way gentlemen went about fighting their contest. The challenge was issued in writing, and could be issued for a variety of reasons, usually involving the honor of those involved (or the reputation of a lady). The letter would list the infraction and demand satisfaction, by either an apology or duel, and was delivered by the best friend of the challenger—these best friends acted as agents and assistants in the duel and were known as 'seconds'. A challenger could also nail his letter in prominent places around town, a process called 'posting'. The challenge could even be placed in the local newspaper. The reply to the challenge was sent in much the same fashion, and these aforementioned best friends would (in theory) attempt to diffuse the source of aggravation between the two parties.

The language used in these challenges is strong and unmistakable in the desire to provoke violence. Consider these excerpts:

"I do declare Seth John Cuthbert to be a coward."

-Wm. McIntosh

"Having received a note from Mr. Henry Putnam by his friend, and having sent an answer thereto by my friend, I do declare said Putnam a coward and not worthy the notice of any gentleman."

-John Wood

"I do proclaim Richard Henry Leake, Attorney-at-Law, to be an infamous liar and vile defamer. Fathers of families, if you value the reputation of your daughters, suffer him not to enter your doors."

-John Miller

"...I therefore pronounce General James Jackson an assassin of reputation and a coward."

-Jacob Waldburger

And often the replies to the challenge were noteworthy as well. A true classic is as follows:

"To the charge of cowardice, I have to reply to Col. John L. Hopkins that I never expect to establish a fair reputation by duelling with men who are unworthy the notice of gentlemen. I am always prepared to repel the assaults of an assassin. You have threatened violence to my person. At your peril make your vaunting true."

-Wm. R. McIntosh

Failing reconciliation by the seconds (often impossible considering the language used in the challenge), the challenged could pick both the place of the duel and the weapons. The challenger would have at least the right of first refusal regarding the choice of weapon, and would have to swear on his honor that he was no expert with the selection by the challenged. The challenger could also pick the distance.

At that point the two parties would meet, and by mutual agreement the firing (or swordplay) would commence—either by signal or gesture. The duel was concluded when honor had been restored by way of apology by the offender, by mutual agreement that honor had been done, or by spilling the blood of an opponent.

Rarely were duels fought to the death. A far more common outcome was the two parties to simply fire a shot in the air and shake hands, something expressly forbidden by European rules but a frequent practice in the States. An accepted end to the duel could also be two exchanges with no blood drawn.

Savannah's Ties to Duelling

No one is certain when the first duel took place in Savannah. The city's founder, James Edward Oglethorpe, was apparently in favor of the practice, asserting at an advanced age that, "Undoubtedly a man has a right to defend his honor." There is no evidence that he was ever forced to thusly defend himself—the most strenuous weapon used outside of actual battle by Oglethorpe was wine, which he threw in retaliation. Oglethorpe did once assert his authority in an impressive yet unusual way in the voyage from England: during a funeral for an infant, who died in transit, one of the potential colonists declared he would throw water on the crowd (for reasons not recorded). Oglethorpe came up behind him and "gave him a good kick on ye arse."

However, the evidence abounds from the early records that there were more than enough duels to go around. Many of the early duels were fought with swords. The duels between Savannahians largely took place across the Savannah River on Hutchinson Island, South Carolina, because of laws which declared such contests a crime. Conversely, many South Carolinians wishing to escape laws restricting that same activity would often have their duels on Tybee Island. Mostly, however, the authorities looked the other way. Duelling was seen as something gentlemen of the period engaged in, and part of a young man's attire was a concealed duelling pistol.

McIntosh vs. Gwinnett

One of the most famous duels in American history was the confrontation between Button Gwinnett, a signer of the Declaration of Independence, and Lachlan McIntosh, fiery patriot. McIntosh's military career started in Georgia at the age of 13. He accompanied his father, a Scotsman, and James Edward Oglethorpe on an expedition into Florida to fight the Spanish. He was captured by the Spaniards in St. Augustine, and was actually taken to Spain and spent years as a prisoner of war. Upon his release he returned to Savannah. He served Oglethorpe as a cadet.

Gwinnett was acting Governor of Georgia during the Revolutionary War. He imagined himself a commander, yet had no military experience. It was General McIntosh, a born military leader, who was in charge of the Continental troops in Georgia. Gwinnett had hoped to be named commander of that same brigade, thus spurring some jealousy between the two men.

Colonial forces in the region often received orders from both Gwinnett and McIntosh that contradicted one another. Their bad relationship was further tainted when an invasion of British- held Florida, planned by Gwinnett, went awry and McIntosh and Samuel Elbert were left wandering around a swamp. McIntosh blamed the mission's failure on Gwinnett. A bad situation got worse when

James Caskey surounded by energy, seen as lighting, strobe light and haze.

McIntosh finally returned to Savannah to find that his brother George had been arrested on charges of treason—by Gwinnett (he was later tried by Congress and released). Both Gwinnett and McIntosh were called in front of a tribunal to explain the failure of the Florida expedition. Gwinnett managed to escape rebuke, but McIntosh was not so lucky. McIntosh had some harsh words with Gwinnett, and Gwinnett challenged him to a duel.

The location of this duel is not known for certain, but it is thought that Gwinnett and McIntosh faced each other in a meadow belonging to Royal Governor James Wright about a mile and a half to the east of the present-day Historic District. The two met, along with their seconds, and agreed to fire from four paces away. They were both wounded in the leg in the exchange. McIntosh's wound was superficial, but Gwinnett was shot just above the knee, a wound that broke his thighbone. McIntosh grimly asked if Gwinnett would like another shot, and Gwinnett answered that he would, if the Seconds would help him to his feet. The Seconds, perhaps not anxious to be in the line of fire between two wounded men with loaded pistols, interceded. Gwinnett died three days later, of a gangrenous infection. McIntosh was tried for murder, but acquitted.

The two combatants are buried about a pistol shot away from each other in Colonial Park Cemetery.

Today, Button Gwinnett is remembered not only for being one of the signers of the Declaration of Independence, but also for the rarity of his signature. Only a few are known to exist. One of these signatures was on a document that was formerly in the possession of the city of Savannah; at least it *was* until an unscrupulous clerk sold it to a collector for $50,000.

Savannahians have had a role as seconds in two of the most famous duels in American history. Nathaniel Pendleton served as second to Alexander Hamilton in his duel with Aaron Burr, and Edward Fenwick Tattnall served in that same capacity for John Randolph in his 1825 contest with Secretary of State Henry Clay.

In Colonial Park Cemetery, there exist reminders of the custom young men made of taking lives because honor demanded it. Odrey Miller, who died in a duel in 1831, has an intriguing gravestone: his friends made sure that the man who shot Odrey Miller was named on his tombstone for posterity. Either Odrey's antagonist or a close friend apparently took exception to the name of Miller's opponent being forever recorded in stone as a killer. Presumably under cover of darkness, he crept into the cemetery and chiseled his name off of Odrey Miller's slab.

Also in Colonial Park is the stone dedicated to James Wilde, a paymaster in the 8th Regiment of the U.S. Army. Wilde fought a duel with a member of his same regiment, Captain R. P. Johnson, and on the fourth exchange, Wilde was struck in the heart. His epitaph includes the words: "...fell in a duel... by the hand of a man who, a short time ago, would have been friendless but for him." He was only twenty-two years old. Wilde's brother, Robert, in the depths of his grief over losing his beloved sibling, wrote a famous verse, considered to be one of the finest American poems ever written:

> *My life is like the summer rose,*
> *That opens to the morning sky;*
> *And ere the shades of evening close,*
> *Is scattered on the ground—to die;*
> *Yet, on that humble bed*
> *The softest dews of night are shed;*
> *As if she wept such a waste to see:*
> *But none shall drop a tear for me.*
>
> *My life is like the autumn leaf,*
> *That trembles in the moon's pale ray;*
> *Its hold is frail, its date is brief—*
> *Restless, and soon to pass away;*
> *Yet when that leaf shall fall and fade,*
> *The parent tree will mourn its shade;*
> *The winds bewail the leafless tree:*
> *But none shall breathe a sigh for me.*
>
> *My life is like the prints, which feet*
> *Have left on Tampa's desert strand;*
> *Soon as the rising tide shall beat,*
> *All trace will vanish from the sand:*
> *Yet, as if grieving to efface*
> *All vestige of the human race,*
> *On that lone shore loud moans the sea:*
> *But none shall thus lament for me.*

In a duel between Patrick Calhoun (grandson of famous politician John C. Calhoun) and J. R. Williamson, the two combatants used five-shot revolvers. Williamson let fly with all his shots in rapid succession, every shot missing the mark. He was defenseless against Calhoun, who still had four bullets left in his arsenal. Calhoun offered clemency by calling out that Williamson could have a chance to offer an apology. Williamson replied, "I have no shot left and you have four. You will have to fire them." Calhoun considered for a moment, and fired his remaining shots in the air. Then the two made a mutual reconciliation.

Sometimes more noteworthy are instances where the planned duel did *not* take place. One such example found its beginning at a dance put on by the Soiree Club. A young Savannah man formerly of South Carolina was turned away at the door because of some minor reason—non-payment of dues or some other infraction. His date was escorted inside by a friend, and the now freshly-single fellow was barred from entry. The young man began to curse, and in the depths of his vitriolic diatribe managed to challenge the Board of Governors to a duel—all *five* of them. The young man had not cooled by morning, and dashed off formal challenges in writing. The Governors of the club reluctantly accepted the challenges, agreeing to fight him one after the other, and each with different weapons: swords, pistols, rifles, shotguns, etc. Fortunately, (especially for the hot-headed young man), the authorities intervened before such a farce could be played out.

There was also a case in point where the two parties were on their way to the duelling ground when the carriage of one of the combatants broke down. The other carriage, carrying the other duellist-to-be, offered help. The repair took some time, and by then it was too late to have their planned duel. The two retired to a house of a mutual friend; they ate supper together, and were forced to share a room together for the night, albeit in different beds. In the morning, they had breakfast together. Then the two proceeded to the duelling ground and exchanged shots, neither coming anywhere near their target. They shook hands, and parted as friends.

And yet another occurrence (or, more properly, a *non*-occurrence) was when the challenged selected the weapon to make a point: double-barreled shotguns loaded with buckshot at twenty paces. The challenger quickly rethought the seriousness of the offense, and dropped his shotgun before the call to fire. Certainly a wise move, considering the spread of the shotgun's blast would have maimed them both.

৯৩Mockery of the Practice৯৩

So many young men were losing their lives in fits of pique that an Anti-Duelling League was formed. But the practice was discontinued not because of the enforcement of laws, or even public outcry. Instead, the strange custom was largely abandoned because of mockery of the duellists themselves by local newspaper editors. The ridicule of duellists started early. Consider this poem excerpt written about the duel between General Howe and General Gadsden, both of the Allied forces in the American Revolution:

> H. missed his mark but not his aim,
> The shot was well-directed;
> It saved them both from hurt and shame,
> What more could be expected?

In the duel, Gadsden's ear was grazed by the shot fired by Howe.

Also critical of duelling was Savannah Morning News editor Joel Chandler Harris, who is famous for his "Uncle Remus" stories. Attributed to Chandler (but possibly another editor) was an amusing anecdote where a visitor to the city became involved in a disagreement with a hotel desk clerk. The two became embroiled in the all-too-familiar exchange of letters precursoring a duel, but the Virginian suddenly apologized to the clerk—and the "popping of pistols... was changed to the popping of corks."

So in this instance, the pen truly did prove mightier than any traditional armament. The last duel was fought between two lawyers in 1877. Depending on the reader's opinion of lawyers, it is either fortunate or unfortunate that the duel was bloodless, and the two former combatants departed on at least fairly friendly terms. Their duel brought to a close the curious practice that Savannah men had engaged in since the beginning of the colony.

In these more modern times, the hot-blooded confrontation has given way to working out disagreements over libations—and thus Savannahians have exchanged one type of shot for another.

Joel Chandler Harris

A few more words are included here about Joel Chandler Harris, whose literary contributions have often been overlooked, especially in this politically-correct climate. A contemporary of Mark Twain, the two often toured the country together, seeing as how they were both Southern writers. The two were also good friends. Mr. Twain had a few humorous words about the first time he met Mr. Harris in his book *Life on the Mississippi* which I will repeat here:

"MR. JOEL CHANDLER HARRIS ('Uncle Remus') was to arrive from Atlanta at seven o'clock Sunday morning; so we got up and received him. We were able to detect him among the crowd of arrivals at the hotel-counter by his correspondence with a description of him which had been furnished us from a trustworthy source. He was said to be undersized, red-haired, and somewhat freckled. He was the only man in the party whose outside tallied with this bill of particulars. He was said to be very shy. He is a shy man. Of this there is no doubt. It may not show on the surface, but the shyness is there. After days of intimacy one wonders to see that it is still in about as strong force as ever. There is a fine and beautiful nature hidden behind it, as all know who have read the Uncle Remus book; and a fine genius, too, as all know by the same sign. I seem to be talking quite freely about this neighbor; but in talking to the public I am but talking to his personal friends, and these things are permissible among friends.

"He deeply disappointed a number of children who had flocked eagerly to Mr. Cable's house to get a glimpse of the illustrious sage and oracle of the nation's nurseries. They said—

"'Why, he's white!'

"They were grieved about it. So, to console them, the book was brought, that they might hear Uncle Remus's Tar-Baby story from the lips of Uncle Remus himself—or what, in their outraged eyes, was left of him. But it turned out that he had never read aloud to people, and was too shy to venture the attempt now. Mr. Cable and I read from books of ours, to show him what an easy trick it was; but his immortal shyness was proof against even this sagacious strategy, so we had to read about Brer Rabbit ourselves."

S avannah Visitors Center on MLK Jr. Blvd.

The Japan Red Cross evinced that it would secede from the Executive Committee for the Consolation of Souls of Dead Chinese POWs, denouncing the latter for being too Leftist-inclined.

—Japanese news item, 1953

On Martin Luther King Jr. Boulevard, there exists a beautiful brick complex which currently houses the Savannah Visitors Center. This sprawling compound is formerly the home of the Central of Georgia Railroad. But some claim it contains echoes from another time, before the railroad and its buildings occupied the spot—an effect still felt today by those sensitive to psychic energy.

Historian Rebecca Clark recalls that on several occasions as a little girl she would experience asthma attacks while at the old train yards. This was puzzling, since she did not have problems with asthma as a general rule, and nowhere else in the city did she suffer from this malady. Her family assumed that she was allergic to some type of flower that perhaps only grew in that part of the city, or because of the wet conditions associated with the area. The site was formerly a swamp known as the Spring Hill Redoubt. But there is significant history associated with that patch of ground.

During the Revolutionary War, the area was the scene of a massive battle. Located on what was then far outside of town, to the southwest, this is where the Allied forces (French, American, and some Haitian troops) fought a desperate melee for control of Savannah on October 9th, 1779. The Allied liberators attacked well-entrenched British forces, who defended the city from invasion in a horseshoe of hastily dug fortifications. These trenches ran through what is today the downtown area—and the Savannah Visitors Center sits on the site of one of the most blood-soaked pieces of ground in the conflict. Close to one thousand men fell in the Siege of Savannah. It was the bloodiest hour of the Revolution— exceeded by only the Battle of Bunker Hill in total dead and wounded. Included in these casualties was Count Casimir Pulaski, who was not only the highest ranking foreign officer to die in the American Revolution, but also considered the Father of the American cavalry. The British ran short of legitimate shot for their cannon, so they resorted to lobbing scrap metal, chains, scissors and anything else they could substitute, and it was with this makeshift ammunition that the Redcoats raked the advancing American soldiers.

In the aftermath of the battle, the Allied forces reached a temporary truce with the British so they could tend to the wounded and bury the dead. These dead were dumped into mass graves near where they fell—and there are reports that some of those men buried were perhaps a little too lively to be categorized as deceased. A local doctor, Dr. Wells, witnessing the aftermath of the battle, recorded that some men were wounded beyond the point of being helped by the crude medicine of the time, so the mortally wounded were piled in with the dead and buried alive.

❧A Claustrophobic Encounter❧

Rebecca Clark recently had lunch at the restaurant at the back side of the Visitors Center, one of only a handful of times she has been back to the old train yard. Perhaps the memory of her childhood fugue had unconsciously contributed to her avoidance of the area. The dining area for the restaurant is located inside an old railroad car, and the property has a courtyard attached, with a bathroom off to one side. It was in this bathroom that Rebecca experienced that familiar shortness of breath—the same tightness of chest that she experienced in nearly the identical spot so many years before. "As soon as I walked into the bathroom I felt it," she says. "It was almost as if there was a heavy weight on my breastbone, making it impossible to breathe." She also could feel shadowy people around her, a feeling she described as "oppressive and weird." Only once she walked from the restroom did the feeling begin to abate.

On a hunch, she walked back into the restaurant and asked about the bathroom—if anyone reported anything strange going on in there. She made no mention of ghosts or any paranormal goings-on, but the waitress looked at her without batting an eyelash and said, "Darlin', that bathroom is haunted. I don't use it." When she pressed for more information, the waitress pointed to Rebecca and called back to the kitchen: "She can feel it, too—it's not just us!"

Rebecca feels that she had a psychic flash from those poor souls being buried alive in the aftermath of the battle. The tightness of her chest and the difficulty breathing may have been a psychic connection to those who would have experienced similar feelings as the dirt was being piled onto them. If it is possible, as explored in other chapters, for a tragic event to bind the spirit of a life cut short to a certain location, then this may explain why several people have experienced strange occurrences at this spot in Savannah. Perhaps, too, the dead object to being buried without a marker or memorial of any kind.

If this last theory is correct, then the fact that Savannah is committed to opening Battlefield Park, a Revolutionary War monument and exhibit grounds may finally put these spirits to rest. This author hopes that their sleep will be more peaceful. At any rate, a commemoration of these brave soldiers who once fought the good fight in an attempt to end British tyranny has been long overdue.

The Foley House

The Foley House Inn, located on Hull Street between Bull & Whitaker Streets, is considered one of the most romantic bed & breakfasts in Savannah. In actuality the luxury inn is contained within two joined structures right off of Chippewa Square. The easternmost of the two was built in 1896—it contains the original inn—and the westernmost was built in 1870.

The Foley House Inn has a bit of strange history associated with it, and it has spawned some folklore. An interview with Charles, a former manager, was an insightful and amusing glimpse at not only the house's history but also the attitude of many residents of the city over Savannah's haunted reputation. Charles confirmed the pertinent information, which is of a forensic nature contained in the story below, and when asked the veracity of the stories told about the Foley House and the city in general, he chuckled.

"I've always thought that Savannah has her reputation because we are a drinking town," he said, "Does the Foley House have a reputation for being haunted? Sure. Have I ever had an experience? No, but then again, I don't drink on the job, either. I've long suspected the housekeepers of taking a nip or two while on the clock—they're the ones always talking about ghosts." He related some of the stories that they have told, including seeing a woman in a white period-style robe in the hallways.

Charles, who thinks the tours in Savannah are often unintentionally funny, related an amusing story in which a carriage tour guide referred to the cast-iron 'dolphin' downspouts as 'mahi mahi spouts', erroneously naming them after the tasty tropical fish instead of the marine mammal. "The guide nearly kicked me off the carriage I was laughing so hard," he explained.

It was for this reason Charles asked only to be included if the following story were told from a historical perspective, meaning it could be told as folklore, and it is recounted here under that condition. Like most folklore, there are bits of fact mixed in—after all, legends must come from somewhere. The following is one version of several different told about the Foley House, with the true facts revealed below:

The structure which would become Foley House was built in 1896 by Honora Foley, who had just suffered the loss of her husband. Her society friends urged her to remarry quickly, since during that time period a woman who had no married by the age of twenty-one was considered a spinster, and Honora was a good deal older, being just past thirty. But Honora refused to entertain thoughts of remarriage simply because of public pressure by well-meaning friends, deciding instead to grieve for her husband until she felt she was ready to love again. During those days there was little a widow could do to support herself, so she opened this home as a boarding house to alleviate the financial burden of being single and began to receive boarders. She promised herself to be very careful to whom she rented a room, because it would be easy to rent a room to the wrong sort of fellow.

One of the first boarders she took in was a gentleman from Tybee Island, whose house had been damaged by a hurricane. Her new renter, Matthew, was a brickmason by trade, and he proved very useful and helpful with many repairs and tasks around the boarding house. The two quickly became friends. Matthew began to volunteer for work, free of charge, around the house where they'd be working side by side, and it became clear that he was attracted to her. He never spoke of it or declared his intentions, being a perfect gentleman, but it was obvious to all that Matthew assisted her with odd jobs simply to spend time with her.

Honora for her part was torn because of his low station in life, and her society friends disapproved. Matthew had none of the wealth or stability that custom deemed right for her. Her relationship with Matthew was never going to progress past friendship unless circumstances changed.

Her next boarder was a gentleman quite different from the first. We'll call him 'Wally'. He was a very attractive man in his early 50's, yet he made her a little uneasy. Honora noticed the way his eyes followed her when she passed in front of him, and she also noticed that he was not such a gentleman as her friend the brickmason. Some of Wally's remarks could be taken in a way that would be inappropriate. Yet, he was a very wealthy man from an even wealthier family. Some of her friends remarked that he would be a much more suitable choice than the brickmason. Still, she felt uncomfortable around him.

Honora spent many days pondering how to reconcile this situation. Wally made his intentions towards her very clear—he wanted a quick courtship and then marriage. He was very attractive, but something about his manner troubled her. He was very unlike her first husband, who had been kind, caring and cautious regarding their finances. It was one of the reasons she still loved her departed dearly: he had cared for her so much that he had made careful investments, explaining that she would be taken care of if something was to ever happen to him. Wally, in contrast, spent money recklessly. He never referenced a job or title, making vague statements or ignoring the question when asked what he did for a living. He also made several casual inquiries about how much she was worth and whether or not she held title to much property. But he was charming and flattering, and her friends were smitten with him.

One night Honora woke up from a sound sleep and realized that *someone was in her room*. She felt herself pinned down to the mattress by strong hands, and then a terrible weight on top of her. Reaching out blindly, she picked up the first object she could grasp—a heavy candlestick holder—and swung it with all of her might. She heard a satisfying thud when it hit home, a grunt, and then the weight fell off of her. When she finally got her senses, she found Wally crumpled by the side of the bed. Wally was very much deceased, his skull dented in at the temple from the candleholder. This is when she realized that her problems had just begun.

Honora had managed to avoid a terrible fate at the hands of Wally, but now she would have to deal with the public inquiry, and worse, lawsuits from Wally's wealthy family. She could even go to prison for murder. Honora's life as she knew it, as well as her fledgling business, was now over. Unless... she did something drastic.

⚘A Foley House Secret⚘

The secret of what happened to Wally took 80 years to spill. The house next door was purchased in the 1960's to expand the Foley House, and a hole was knocked into the wall separating the two structures. As the wall came down, Wally literally spilled out at the feet of the workmen. They had uncovered a false wall, expertly built, added into the Foley House to conceal the body. Honora Foley had apparently had one more odd-job for her brickmason, which he obviously carried out with all the skill of a master builder. The addition was so artfully done, no one suspected a thing for 82 years.

Of course, Wally was not his real name, but what better to call a man who spent so many years sealed in a wall?

Women often report a chill when standing near where the false wall used to stand. Wally apparently still makes his presence known in this fashion.

Our mason Matthew apparently had a fee for his services: he and Honora were married and lived in perfect harmony, as best we can tell, for over thirty years. Nothing like a shared secret to cement a romance. Matthew had sealed the deal. However, it could be argued that Honora exchanged one ball and chain for another.

The folklore fills in the story surrounding the facts, and does so in an amusing way, like so many legends. The pertinent facts are these: Honora Foley, recent widow, did indeed build the Foley House in 1896. Years later, when the Bed &Breakfast was being expanded, the wall separating the structures was torn down, and a body was found, in the words of the manager Charles, "*Very* dead." However, no clue has emerged as to the man's identity.

Is the elaborate story of Honora, Wally and Matthew true? Probably not. But it is one more legend that really should be true, and no one in Savannah would be surprised if it were.

Savannah Theatre

The Savannah Theatre on Chippewa Square is the oldest continuously operating theatre in the United States, opening in December, 1818. Originally designed by William Jay as a Regency style structure, the theatre has burned several times during its history, which explains the theatre's current Art Deco façade. Enough of the original theatre remains even after the fires that the theatre can still lay claim to the title of America's oldest operating playhouse.

The opening night featured a double bill, with the comedy 'The Soldier's Daughter' and the farce 'Raise the Wind' playing to a sold-out crowd. Many complaints were made about the ladies in the audience having hairstyles so tall that they blocked the view of the action. The *Georgian* newspaper reported the next morning that the ladies' piled-high hair "might be mistaken for steeple of the new brick church," a reference to the newly-completed Independent Presbyterian Church on nearby Oglethorpe Avenue.

☜A Revealing Ghost☞

The theatre also has its share of unscheduled performances of the spectral kind. A Savannah Morning News article from 1895 relates several fantastic accounts of ghosts in the old playhouse. In one instance, a mysterious fire burned a hole in the floor of one of the dressing rooms, but singed nothing else and, just as curiously, put itself out.

The paper goes on to say that several police officers on various occasions, both on foot patrol and on horseback, reported hearing a strange noise in the wee hours of the morning near the old theatre. Even though the theatre was clearly deserted, the officers claimed to hear applause coming from the empty playhouse. None of these officers appeared brave enough to investigate, because no official report was ever made about the strange sounds of merriment coming from the old theatre.

But by far the strangest account was that which occurred in the Green Room, which is a rehearsal room near the McDonough St. side of the theatre. A group of female dancers who were using this room to change into their costumes suddenly felt a sensation of being watched by someone or something unseen. They described this presence as unspeakably malevolent and evil. So strong was this overpowering feeling of dread that they fled the dressing room in various stages of undress! One can only imagine the incredible sight of a gaggle of screaming, scantily-clad ladies running for the exit— and one also wonders if the show in which they were performing could possibly approach the unbelievable scene of the near-naked cast fleeing en mass to McDonough St. So this is one case where the ghost's performance—and the reaction of the 'co-stars'—surely overshadowed the real production.

The theatre also made national headlines in 1906, when a suspicious fire broke out several nights before Thomas Dixon's controversial play 'The Clansman' was supposed to be performed. It is widely suspected that the Ku Klux Klan started the blaze.

When the theatre was being remodeled in the early part of the 20th century, a portion of a brick wall, upon being broken, was found to contain a penny from 1818. Apparently it had been left in the wall by a worker constructing the original theatre. It was subsequently carried by the then-owner of the theatre, Fred Weis as a good-luck charm for many years. Weis lost the penny while in New York in 1948, and the Savannah Theatre almost immediately had a fire which nearly reduced it to embers.

～A Notorious Actor～

A few other instances of strange history surround the old playhouse. In the 1850's, actor John Wilkes Booth performed at the Savannah Theatre. Booth would go on to assassinate U.S. President Abraham Lincoln in Washington, D.C., in April of 1865.

Coincidentally, there is another connection between the Booth and Lincoln families. In 1863, the eldest son of Abraham Lincoln, Robert, was standing on a railway platform in Trenton, New Jersey, two full years before his father was assassinated. The crowd surged forward, and the son of the President was knocked onto the tracks and was about to be killed by a train. An onlooker reached down from the crowd and pulled the young Lincoln to safety. That onlooker's name was *Edwin* Booth, the famous actor and brother of John Wilkes Booth. So famous was Edwin that Robert immediately recognized the face of his favorite actor, thanking him profusely. The two maintained a friendship for the rest of their lives, even though that terrible tragedy took place between their families in 1865 at Ford's Theatre.

So in this instance, the older brother Booth saved the son, but the younger brother shot the father.

There are other curious oddities involving Robert Todd Lincoln and presidential assassins: not only was he at his father's side when he passed away, but years later, as Secretary of War, Todd Lincoln was present and ready to meet President James A Garfield, when Garfield was assassinated in 1881. And, in 1901, when Todd Lincoln entered the Pan-American Exposition Hall in Buffalo, NY, President William McKinley was assassinated, as well.

McDonough's Restaurant

McDonough's Restaurant, located across McDonough Street from the Savannah Theatre, is definitely a locals' hangout. The place combines offbeat locals and a steady tourist crowd, and also mixes a traditional Irish pub with a more modern karaoke bar (consistently voted best in the city) and dance floor. Among its virtues are a full late-night menu that serves until 2:30 a.m., and a happy hour that runs from 8 a.m. to 8 p.m. It seemingly has captured the flavor of Savannah like no other bar, which is not surprising, given the history of the location. According to the owner of the bar, the structure also houses its share of things that go bump—or crash—in the night.

Researching property in Savannah to find out when a structure was built can sometimes be frustrating, but also there are times when the confusion generated by contradicting records can sometimes reveal a wonderful story. McDonough's is a perfect example of this. According to property records kept by the Chatham County Board of Assessors, the building was built in two stages: the northern side came first, in 1890, and the southern side was an addition in 1900. But the records at the Georgia Historical Society contradict these dates. Since the GHS records are generally seen as more reliable, the archives housed there will usually clear up any doubt. Not so in the case of when the structure housing McDonough's was built; in fact, the archives deepen rather than solve the mystery. According to the property documents, the lot was given in 1831 to the Unitarian Society by the mayor and aldermen. The lot was sold numerous times between then and 1854, which is where we have any record of a structure being built by Dr. J. Gordon Howard—and apparently it took 2 years to build. Shoddy record-keeping can perhaps be explained by the South's plunge into the War Between the States from 1861- 65. And that brings us to an intriguing character.

⚬⁓The Curiosity Shop ⁓⚬

In 1867, the building was owned by Theodore Meves, who opened a museum that he called the 'Curiosity Shop'. The museum had exhibits of shells, minerals, and exotic animals. Meves advertised that his museum's admission was fifty cents, and twenty-five cents for children, and he would often put on shows where he would feed rats to rattlesnakes. He advertised that he had the World's Smallest Cow, and also claimed to have an alligator, rare birds, and a lion cub that was teething. He was sued by his neighbor for keeping and feeding a she-bear on his property, and won a settlement in the suit. The next year, probably much to the chagrin of his neighbor, he advertised a 'Bear Fight'—no word on who or what the bear was opposing in the contest. One must wonder if the opponent was human, and if so, did Meves wish it was his cranky neighbor?

Meves was also a member of the German Friendly Society, and was skilled at the art of fireworks, being employed by the city numerous times for that purpose. Records are incomplete as to when Meves moved his museum to Monterey Square, but by 1870, we know that it had been converted into a grocery store by Julius Koox. In the historical records at GHS, we find that it is the southern addition, and not the northern part of present-day McDonough's which was built between 1890- 94. The tax records also state that there is confusion about the roof addition as well, but the office space was added sometime between 1919- 24.

Over the years the brick building housed many things, but in 1987 it was bought by owner Billy Lee, who converted it into an Irish pub.

✎A Revealing Interview✎

Mr. Lee graciously took several hours out of his busy schedule to relate his strange experiences in the old structure. In 1991, he says, he was living in the apartment on the second floor, located above the bar, and this is when things began to get odd.

He began to hear unexplained noises. "From my old bedroom, you can look out the door and adjoining the living room area there's a galley-style kitchen. That kitchen area is where I heard most of the noises. Sometimes I would hear pots and pans clanking, and other times I would hear a crash in the kitchen. Sometimes I would hear boards creaking, like someone was walking around. The first time it happened, I thought I had a prowler, so I actually drew my pistol and went to investigate. Of course, nothing was there." Oddly (or perhaps not, considering Savannah's haunted reputation), this is not the only instance of a gun being drawn in response to a supernatural happening.

Mr. Lee had frequent encounters with his less-than-quiet unwanted spirit. "It got to be a common happening around there," he explains, "And it didn't seem to matter if I was alone or not. I had a girlfriend at the time who was terrified of the sounds that would come out of that kitchen at all hours of the night. She refused to come over to my apartment, because she was afraid of ghosts and wanted nothing to do with it. I could visit her, but spending the night at my place was out of the question." Mr. Lee apparently took exception to having his social life infringed upon, because he began to attempt to rid himself of the ghost. "I yelled at it," he says sheepishly. "The funny thing is, it seemed to work. The incidents fell off after that, so I guess it got the message. Things would still happen, but not nearly as much as before."

Later, Billy Lee began to have very different experiences on the third floor. "This was a different type of ghost altogether," he said. "My friend noticed it first. We were sitting on the couch watching television, and suddenly she asked, 'What was that?' I didn't know what she meant, so she explained that she had seen some sort of gold light zip by, starting at the stairs. And I'll be darned if I didn't start seeing it, too, from time to time. It was this little slice of golden light which would zip right by. I saw it by the stairs, and I also saw it in the bathroom. It was the strangest thing—until you actually see something like that which you can't explain, you can never understand." It must be noted that Mr. Lee's arms had broken out in goosebumps at this point in the interview. He did not appear to notice, and continued his story.

"I just get the feeling that this was a child. The light was only about four feet off the ground, right about the height of a child, and I don't know, just something about it made me think of someone very young. Maybe it's the energy or speed at which this light moves at—it's like a dervish, then it's gone." When asked if perhaps something tragic had happened in the buildings past involving a child, Mr. Lee says, "I've never found any record of anything like that, but this is a very old building. You never know, do you?"

Indeed, the history of an old building often resembles a half-completed puzzle even when a lot of records have been kept. Clear enough to make out the overall picture, but many details are missing. Keeping with the 'jigsaw puzzle' analogy, for a structure like McDonough's where so much is unresolved already, the story of the strange hauntings on the second and third floors must remain thus far unassembled. The chapter of who or what haunts the building remains unwritten, for now.

McDonough's is open from 8 a.m. to 3 a.m., and serves food until 2:30 a.m.

Andrew Low House

On the southwest trust lot of Lafayette Square is the Andrew Low House, which is today a beautiful house museum. The residence was completed in 1849 by John S. Norris, a noted architect responsible for much of the wondrous structures being erected during that time period. The house combines Greek revival elements along with unusually square proportions and deep bracketed eaves—which speak of Italianate influences. A pair of imposing cast-iron lions guards the front door.

Built for British cotton merchant Andrew Low, the house is run today by the Colonial Dames of America in the State of Georgia. The carriage house is a museum run by the Girl Scouts of Savannah. Low originally married a local, Sarah Cecilia Hunter, but both she and the couple's four year old son died before the house was completed. Low remarried 5 years after their death to Mary Cowper Stiles, and had a son and three daughters. The son, William Mackay Low, would marry Juliette Gordon, eventual founder of the Girl Scouts.

Low was a Confederate sympathizer; he saw the Confederacy as a valuable and profitable trading partner with England. In 1862, Low and his wife were arrested in the North while returning from England. Andrew Low was accused of being a Confederate collaborator and spy because of an intercepted message that identified a Confederate agent in England named Low. The couple did nothing to deny this, and the Union officials spent weeks sorting out the confusion. Andrew Low was imprisoned in Boston on suspicion of collaborating with the enemy. According to family lore, Mrs. Low, then pregnant, hid incriminating papers and letters in her coiled hairstyle to protect her husband. It turned out that John Low (the brother-in-law of Andrew Low's business partner, Charles Green) was the real agent, and the confusion enabled him to slip safely back to Savannah before the Federals realized their mistake.

The Low family was renowned for their hospitality. Prominent English author William Makepeace Thackeray recorded his feelings in a letter written in one of the guest bedrooms: "Know that I write from the most comfortable quarters I have ever had in the United

States. In a tranquil old city, wide stretched, tree-planted, with a few cows and carriages toiling through the sandy road, a red river with a tranquil little fleet of merchant men taking cargo, and tranquil warehouses barricaded with packs of cotton; a famous good dinner, breakfast, etc. and leisure all morning to think and do and sleep and read as I like. The only place I say in the States where I can get these comforts - all free gratis- is in the house of my friend Andrew Low of the great house of A. Low and Co., Cotton Dealers, brokers."

Juliette Gordon Low was born on October 31st, 1860. As a child, she was stopped on the street by friend of her mother's, who commented that she was a pretty little girl. "No I'm not," she protested, "My Mama says I'm as ugly as ten bears!" Daisy at the age of eight allowed a cousin to braid taffy into her hair, and had to have it cut out when it hardened.

This eccentric behavior did not diminish with age. She was sometimes seen wearing live vegetables on her hat in place of flowers, and once went trout fishing with Rudyard Kipling in full evening dress. And she was never good with money—she was constantly borrowing money from friends and acquaintances. Her idea to solve this problem was to sew silver dollars into her belt so she would always have an extra bit of money in case she ran short.

Andrew's son William married Juliette Gordon Low in 1886. An omen of their marriage occurred right after the ceremony. Juliette had a grain of good-luck rice lodge in her good ear, virtually destroying her hearing. She did not let this misfortune deter her, however; to talk with Daisy was to have her dominate the conversation anyway.

Her marriage to William was an unhappy one, and their union fell apart in 1901. She spent the next decade traveling about the world, searching for fulfillment. She met Sir Robert Baden-Powell in 1911 in England, who founded the Boy Scouts. Baden-Powell was mortified when 6,000 *girls* applied for the Boy Scouts. He urged Daisy to pursue a sister organization for the Scouts, and so Daisy became involved in organizing the Girl Guides in England and Scotland. She eventually introduced the Guides to America, starting in Savannah. The first troop was founded in Savannah on March 12th, 1912.

By the time of her death in 1927, the Girl Scouts of America organization had grown to nearly 168,000 members. She was buried in her Girl Scout uniform—and in her pocket was a telegram from the Girl Scout National Council, delivered right before her death: "You are not only the first Girl Scout but the best Girl Scout of them all."

৵Storied Past, Supernatural Present৶

A house with such involvement in the historic course of events in Savannah would surely have a few supernatural stories to tell. Mostly, sounds and shadows are reported in the old house. One housekeeper has said she has seen the blonde apparition of Mary Cowper Stiles, whom she refers to as 'Miss Mary', on numerous occasions. It must be a frequent happening, judging from the first-name familiarity. The housekeeper has said that Miss Mary is often sad because of her lost children.

Mary died in the master bedroom, where Juliette Gordon Low also passed away. Former tour guide Missy Brandt reported always having a strange feeling in that bedroom. "You never feel like you're alone," she said.

Missy also recounted the time she was mistaken for a ghost. She recounts walking in the lower floors of the house museum, and one of the docents caught sight of her shadow and a glimpse of her blonde hair and nearly had a heart attack. The woman grabbed her chest and gasped. "I was afraid that I had made a ghost," Missy joked, "But fortunately she survived."

Missy also recounted hearing footsteps near her office. They came from the direction of the old butler's pantry, so the phantom footsteps are thought to belong to 'Old Tom', the lifelong servant for the Low family.

Perhaps the ghosts in the old house have an appreciation for the hard work done by the Andrew Low House's fine staff. It would stand to reason that such historically important characters that shaped Savannah's past would have an affinity for continuing their spectral existence in a proper setting. Maybe such cultured and respected individuals have retained their good taste—in the spirit world.

The Andrew Low House, at 329 Abercorn Street, is open to the public: Monday-Saturday 10:30 am - 3:30 pm; Sundays 12:00 - 3:30 pm Closed on Thursdays and National Holidays.

Girl Scout First Headquarters, on 330 Drayton St, is open Monday, Tuesday, Friday and 1ˢᵗ and 3ʳᵈ Saturdays from 10 am to 4 pm.
For tour appointments: (912) 232-8200, or fax (912) 236-9796

Hamilton-Turner Inn

On the southeastern side of Lafayette Square, the Hamilton-Turner Mansion represents one of the finest examples of the Second French Empire style of architecture in the United States. It was built in 1873 for wealthy jeweler and businessman Samuel P. Hamilton. Hamilton was not only a jeweler but was also the president of the electric company and the mayor. One of the richest men in town, he wanted to showcase his wealth, and the house certainly accomplished that goal. The Hamilton-Turner Inn was one of the first homes in Savannah to have electricity; a crowd gathered when the switches were thrown for the first time, because some were convinced that the house would explode. Hamilton is reputed to have left the lights blazing at all hours, even all night long, possibly to irritate his neighbor, who was the president of the gas company. The windows are single panes, which was incredibly expensive because it was a fairly new technology at that time.

As the owner of the largest and most opulent house in town (and during the time of Reconstruction), Mr. Hamilton was fearful of thieves breaking in and stealing his valuables. To guard against break-ins, he hired an off-duty policeman to stand guard on the roof with a rifle. His plan literally backfired, however: the guard was found early one morning in a pool of blood, shot down from his perch atop the house. No one was ever charged in the murder, and the slaying has gone unexplained to this day. Hamilton himself died in 1899.

Many claim that the house served as the model for Disney's Haunted Mansion attraction, but the theme park house was actually inspired by an existing structure located in Baltimore, Maryland. There is no connection between the Hamilton-Turner House and the Haunted Mansion attraction. The house does resemble the artwork of *New Yorker* Magazine cartoonist Charles Addams—indeed; older Savannah residents will sometimes call the mansion "the Charles Addams House."

⁊A *Midnight* Connection⁊

Along with the beautiful architecture, the house also draws some attention from those seeking the locations mentioned in the bestseller *Midnight in the Garden of Good and Evil*, because it was owned by Nancy Hillis, the character known as "Mandy" in the book. This was also the location of Joe Odom's ostensible museum and house tour. Ms. Hillis owned the mansion for a number of years, and rented out rooms to make ends meet. As reported in the History Channel's 'Haunted History-Savannah' program, the first incident that happened while Hillis owned the structure was witnessed by a tenant, who saw a man standing at the top of the stairs. He was described as a man wearing a smartly-tailored suit, and his features match that of Samuel P. Hamilton.

Hillis herself reported hearing footsteps running on the upper floors on numerous occasions. She, along with a friend, was so alarmed by this that they even dialed the police in one instance. Upon arrival, the Savannah police officer also confirmed that he heard the footsteps, and went upstairs to investigate. All he found were empty rooms, and all the points of entry or exit were locked.

⁊Some Ghosts Have a Ball⁊

But by far the most common hauntings at the Hamilton-Turner Mansion have to do with Mr. Hamilton's children. As a wealthy and powerful socialite, Hamilton would throw grand parties. It has been said that Mr. Hamilton asked his children to steer clear of these social galas, and the two children would stay in the upper floor and play billiards. Apparently these children grew bored with their game, or at least bored from being excluded from the fun downstairs time and time again. They began first rolling, then *throwing* the billiard balls down the stairs to break up the monotony. It is this sound that is sometimes still heard coming from the upper floors of the old house.

"I've heard pool balls 'breaking'"—meaning racked balls being put into play—"and I've heard them rolling down the stairs," claims one former innkeeper. "I've even heard giggling coming from the top floor."

This same innkeeper had a strange brush with yet another ghost on the property. As she was heading out to her car on Lafayette Square one night near dusk, she experienced a feeling of being watched. "I looked back at the house, thinking perhaps someone had called me, and that's when something caught my eye. I saw a man's silhouette standing motionless on the roof. As I stood there, thinking I was seeing things, I realized I could see a faint orange glow of the man's cigar. I blinked a couple of times, and then he was gone. Vanished, in front of my own two eyes."

Was this the ghostly sentry, still watching over the house? Does he feel as though his duty to guard the Mansion is still incomplete? And what of the children—are they the Hamilton children, still bored and wanting some attention?

Only one thing is certain: you would be hard-pressed to find a more luxurious inn in which to experience a haunting.

215 E. Charlton St. Poltergeist

I believe... that those apparitions and ghosts of departed persons are not the wandring souls of men, but the unquiet walks of Devils, prompting and suggesting us unto mischief, blood and villainy; instilling and stealing into our hearts that the blessed Spirits are not at rest in their graves, but wander solicitous of the affairs of the World.

—Browne
Religio Medici

Researching ghost stories can give one a reputation, earned or not, for being knowledgeable in all aspects of the supernatural. Sometimes that reputation can spawn some odd questions.

"How do you get rid of a ghost?" The young man asking was quite serious, and as absurd as the question was at face value, in

Savannah this is a pertinent query. The exasperated fellow in question had exhausted every patience to try to quell the strange happenings. Roger went on to tell a story about his new apartment, located at 215 East Charlton St., one in a perfect location right off of Lafayette Square. The house itself was built in 1889 by Captain James Johnston. A carriage house existed on the property before that time.

☞Bloody Plot☜

The house's history reveals no clue as to the apparently violent entity inhabiting its walls. But perhaps the strange haunting has more to do with the history of the land on which the structure sits. Before the house was built, the area was involved in the Siege of Savannah, which was the second bloodiest battle of the American Revolution.

On September 8th, 1779, a French fleet comprised of 42 vessels appeared off the coast. They were commanded by Count Charles-Henri d'Estaing, who had brought with him a force of four thousand French, Irish, and black volunteers from Haiti. Their goal was to wrest British-occupied Savannah away from the Crown and restore it to American rule. The troops converged on Savannah, and were met by nearly 1,000 American soldiers from Charleston and Augusta. Included among the Americans were Colonel Francis Marion, later known as the Swamp Fox, Sergeant William Jasper, hero of Charleston, and Count Casimir Pulaski.

D'Estaing called for the surrender of the British, commanded by General Prevost (nicknamed 'Old Bullet Head' for an old wound to his temple). Prevost asked for a 24-hour truce to consider his options, and then used that time to fortify his positions. At the end of the 24 hours, General Prevost sent his reply—they would fight. Amazingly, d'Estaing did not attack immediately, instead laying siege to the city for 3 weeks.

The French artillery can be excused for their inaccuracy: a mistake by the ship's steward called for each cannon crew to receive a keg of rum instead of a keg of beer. The cannon batteries bombarded the city's houses, the public buildings, and on occasion their own troops— in fact they hit everything except the enemy. A terrified population sought refuge with their captors after being bombarded by their so-called liberators. A number of women and children were killed in the barrage. Some children established a cottage industry: snuffing out the French cannonballs with sand and selling them to the British, so they could be fired back.

Without reinforcements, the British had no hope of holding out. Fortunately for them, British Colonel John Maitland, with his 800 troops, slipped past French sentries and relieved the beleaguered city. It was then that d'Estaing launched his attack, which was in theory a surprise assault, but in actual practice was anything but.

The attack was to take place in the very early morning hours of October 9th. The British were warned well in advance by civilians, which were allowed free movement between the Allied battle lines and the town. The attackers were pounded by artillery from both land and sea. The attempted assault lasted just an hour, the bloodiest hour of the entire Revolution. D'Estaing himself was wounded twice. Among the dead was Count Casimir Pulaski, who was the highest-ranking foreign officer to die in the Revolution, and Sergeant William Jasper, who was killed trying to save his regimental colors.

Overall, there were nearly 1,000 casualties, most of them Allied. The battle clearly over, a truce was called, and the bodies of the dead were buried in an unmarked mass grave, the location of which is unknown. The Allies retreated, and Savannah would remain in English hands until July 11th, 1782.

Years later, during the French Revolution, D'Estaing was condemned to beheading by guillotine. He stated, "When you cut off my head, send it to the British, for they shall pay you handsomely for it!"

Perhaps, as has been explored in other chapters, the energy from past events can literally become embedded in a specific location. What then, of this unassuming house on a peaceful square? If accounts of the battle which occurred here are accurate, then the plot of ground upon which the house is built was literally soaked with blood. This small area has seen perhaps as much pain and suffering as any spot on the planet. The screams of the wounded, groans of the dying, and roar of the cannon would have drowned out the curses of the Allied troops towards their incompetent commanders.

∽Roger's Encounters∽

Perhaps this violent past explains Roger's experiences in his new apartment. The spectral activity started right away, after he had moved into his new ground-level apartment. As people often do, he had unpacked his picture frames and art prints onto the floor along the baseboard, trying to figure out where best to hang them. While talking to a friend who was helping him unpack his kitchen supplies, he began leaning against the kitchen doorframe. Suddenly he felt a hand in the center of his chest that pushed him backwards with surprising force. He stepped back to regain his balance and stepped right through a glass picture frame, cutting his foot badly in the process. He and his friend had not been drinking at all, he says, and the friend was shocked at how forcefully he was hurled backwards.

"I'm a grown man and I'm scared of this," he said with conviction. But the most disturbing aspect of Roger's haunting has come during the nighttime hours. His peaceful slumber has been nothing of the sort. He has awakened on numerous occasions to find himself being pushed violently out of bed! He swears he isn't dreaming—he didn't fall, but has rather been pushed roughly out of bed in the wee hours of the morning. One night he was shoved with so much violent force that he hit the wall, some two feet away, before slamming down to the ground. Roger was dazed by the incident. It is unlikely that Roger, even rolling in his sleep as hard as he could muster, could do this. The only conclusion possible is that he was slammed out of bed by something with the force of a football linebacker smashing an offensive lineman.

This was apparently Roger's breaking point (pardon the pun), and it prompted the aforementioned question that gave this author pause. The admittedly unqualified advice given by this author was that these are classic symptoms of what is known as a poltergeist (German for 'noisy ghost'). Poltergeists are flare-ups of pent up energy, and can manifest themselves as doors slamming, objects breaking, or as experienced by Roger, can sometimes unfortunately direct their energy towards an individual.

The first step taken in dealing with an unwanted poltergeist is also the easiest: ask it to leave, in a firm voice. If that fails, one may call in a priest or minister to bless the house, or even perform an exorcism. The last step would be to simply move.

This may be the answer for poor Roger, who is still having incidents up until the time of this writing. A mutual acquaintance of Roger's and this author remarked recently that he had more trouble in the middle of the night: he was hurled out of bed with enough force to bruise his wrist.

One can only hope that Roger can find either peace with the entity occupying his home, or devise a successful strategy for driving out his unwanted 'friend'. Considering the military history of the plot—and its unfamiliarity with the phrase 'successful strategy'— Roger may want to pursue a truce with the violent spirit whose space he shares. Or, simply withdraw.

Presence at 441 Barnard St.

In a lovely three story 1860 townhouse located on Barnard Street, several odd supernatural occurrences have been noted. The structure's calm exterior and happy current residents belie a deeply troubling melancholy which permeates the home. A presence has been felt by several people, including both a current owner, as well as by this author, in 1998.

I was recently out of art school, and was making a decent living as a decorative and portrait painter. I was referred to my new clients at 441 Barnard Street by an interior decorator. Right away, I hit it off with my prospective clients—my ideas seemed to mesh exactly with what the couple envisioned for their home. One small project suddenly became many, including a few large-scale decorative works. I painted a floor to look like marble, and did some faux finishes—including woodgraining and faux brickwork. The clients seemed very happy with my work, and began to treat me like a member of the family, albeit a well-paid one. I often listened to music as I worked, and the couple and I found that even our musical tastes coincided, so I began at their request to unplug the headphones and let the music play. We all seemed to enjoy the old greats, like Nina Simone, Billie Holliday, Louis Armstrong, and even more modern favorites such as Clapton and Billy Joel.

Several of the projects were large-scale enough that I needed to stay late, and the couple became accustomed to leaving me in their house while they attended parties and dinners, always just telling me to lock up behind myself and drop the key through the mail slot when I left. One night, leaving to attend a society function, my patrons left me behind in their living room working high up on a ladder. My CD player had been switched off while they had been talking on the phone earlier in the evening, and I remember quite vividly taking the CD out of the player and placing it back in the jewel case. As the shadows grew darker, and I grew closer and closer to finishing, I had an experience that I will never forget—and to this day just the thought gives me chills: I began to hear slow, sad music beneath me. The CD player had turned on by itself. At first I thought I was imagining it. And yet, Nina Simone's sultry voice issued forth, incredibly singing from the mix CD I had removed from the player, and it wasn't the first song in the queue she sang; but the third. There was no way not to take it personally—I felt that this song had been selected because of its specific lyrics.

> *I put a spell on you*
> *'Cause you're mine*
>
> *You better stop the things you do*
> *I ain't lyin'*
> *No I ain't lyin'*

Needless to say, I stopped the things I was doing. I stop quoting the lyrics at that point because that is how far I heard Nina get in her song. I am unsure if she got any farther, because I ran about as fast as I've ever run before, and I'm a former college baseball player. I fled as a man chased by bees must run, grabbing the key as I ran past the table by the front door, locking up and *throwing* the key through the mail slot below before running again to my car. Only then I stopped, panting, and then and only then did I wonder if there was any logical explanation to what had transpired. Could the couple be putting me on somehow? Was it a joke? Or had I just had a strange encounter with something I couldn't explain? But I didn't let that thought linger, as I put the car into drive.

With some trepidation, I went to work the next morning. The lady of the house was fixing coffee as I entered timidly. Everything was as I had left it the night before, including one of my prized brushes, which I had left loaded with paint so the bristles had dried in an ugly glob. I opened my CD player and saw what I had suspected—

the player was indeed empty. The CD was snug in the jewel case. I asked her if she or her husband had been listening to any music, and she said, "No, we like our mornings pretty quiet... no music or TV before ten or so."

She went on: "I thought you were getting close to being finished with that project last night... did you get tired?" I told her that I hadn't felt very inspired the previous night, and left pretty quickly— in fact that was the truth. Nothing could uninspire me quite like what may have been a message from a ghost. I watched her carefully to see if she or her husband appeared to be having fun at my expense, but saw no guile in their expressions.

Just as casually as I could manage, I asked, "Is this place haunted?" She didn't even pause in her pouring of the coffee: "Oh, yes. I feel the presence sometimes in the late evenings. My husband doesn't agree—," he ruffled his morning paper right on cue—"but I often feel like there's a black girl... a cook, maybe... in here from a long time ago. I've even seen her a few times," she said earnestly, "Or at least I see a quick flash out of the corner of my eye and then she's gone."

She went on to explain that she sometimes got the impression of a deep, silent sadness as the shadows lengthened into gloom. Nothing ever overt, just an impression of someone who had a bitter place in her heart.

I never explained what had happened the previous night, but I am pretty sure they could tell that something had transpired. I suppose I was afraid of losing them as clients—at the time I did not yet research ghosts and tell ghost stories for a living. I still considered people who believed in ghosts to be slightly off, and was worried that they might assume the same. I never had the opportunity to work late into the evening in the upstairs ever again, as my project moved me into a different area of the house, complete with different hours. But the question has always lingered since that strange happening: what could have caused that CD player to turn on by itself and play music with no CD inside? A check of the townhouse's history reveals no likely suspects in the search for the mystery woman seen and sensed by the lady of the house.

If it was indeed a message from beyond, what did it mean? Nina Simone's song is about a woman at the end of her rope: she's torn up inside by a man who cheats, yet she still loves him. Was this spirit relating to the lyrics? Perhaps the message expressed in Nina Simone's old song could be truly universal.

✍ The Downstairs Presence ✍

After my work in the upstairs was completed, I was asked to work in the downstairs apartment. The floors, my patron couple explained, were concrete, and they planned on using area rugs throughout that level in the house. Wouldn't faux marble look wonderful in between the rugs? At twenty-four dollars an hour I couldn't have agreed more.

Unfortunately, the only part of my plan I hadn't considered was that the only time a floor painter can work is when his surface is dry to the touch, and the paint had a drying time of six hours, which meant I'd be working all sorts of strange times. Working alone at all hours of the night is never comfortable, but in Savannah the 'witching hour' can often take on a whole new meaning. I began to hear things— I often heard disembodied footsteps as I labored on the floor. Understand that I knew I was all alone in the area, but nevertheless I could hear and feel someone near. In one notable instance, I heard the distinct heavy tread of someone come down the outside stairs from the townhouse above, pause on the sidewalk, and then walk towards the open door of the downstairs in which I was working. I raised my eyes to ask a question to either of my two employers, and the question died on my lips. I was completely alone.

On another occasion, a slithery scratching sound worked its way down the back door. Thinking one of my upstairs patrons needed something, I opened the back door, and no one was there.

I mentioned the strange noises once to a plumber who had come to work on the toilet in the downstairs bathroom. He not so politely told me that perhaps I should open a window or two, because the paint fumes were obviously getting to me. But I was not the only one to hear them. A contractor who came in to do some electrical work turned to me and said, "I don't know how you can stay here all hours of the night. I hear people who aren't there walking around all the time down here."

Photographs taken of the space by this author reveal a myriad of strange orbs and lights. My intention was not to capture anything out of the ordinary—I was simply attempting to photograph my work—and the photos were taken before I had even heard of orb photography. It took several tries with the digital camera to get a photo of the space *without* some odd floating orbs appearing in the frame. It wasn't until years later that I realized what had been captured in the photos.

I began to wonder who exactly would be staying in this haunted space—more specifically wondering who would stay for long. One afternoon I got my answer: the lady of the house came down to check my progress, and mentioned that the space was going to be a short-term rental space only. Specifically the downstairs would be rented to doctors, who come from out of town for short stays at a local hospital from one to four weeks.

I remember musing to myself at the time that the doctors had better be *cardiologists*.

The Slave & Geechee Culture

All Negroes... who are now or shall hereafter be in this province and all their issue and offspring Born or to be Born shall be and they are hereby declared to be and remain hereafter absolute slaves and shall follow the condition of the mother and shall be deemed in law to be chattels personal in the hands of their owners and possessors.

- Georgia's slave code of 1755

The record of slavery in the South is not a particularly gentle one, nor is it a proud moment in American history. Originating in Africa, where slavery itself was common, a person could be bought or traded for, and shipped to the Americas by slavers. Often, the ones doing the enslaving were rival African tribes—selling prisoners of war was a common practice. An account of the despicable practice can be found in the section detailing the voyage of the renegade slave ship *Wanderer*, contained in this volume.

In addition to codes enforcing slavery as an accepted condition, there were also laws concerning things not allowed, as well. Slaves were not allowed to own a dog or a gun, sell liquor or assemble for any purpose other than religious worship. It was against the law to teach a slave to read or write. A slave could not be out on the streets after eight p.m. And yet there was a burgeoning social order forming amongst those ensnared in the one hundred ten years of legalized slavery in Savannah.

The Geechee culture in the area is a remnant from what was once this society of slaves. Often times, this culture is mistakenly called 'Gullah', but in actuality the Gullah people exist in an area to the north, in and around Charleston, South Carolina. The two peoples are similar, but not interchangeable: both are rooted in slavery, but the Geechee people have a history and tradition all their own.

Freed after the Civil War, these Island people would often group near the coast where both fishing and farming was plentiful. Named after the Ogeechee River, the community developed their own dialect—one similar to the pronunciations elucidated in Joel Chandler Harris's *Uncle Remus* stories. In addition to what amounted to their own language (also called 'Geechee', or 'Geech' for short), this culture also had an elaborate belief system through their African descent that stretched back before the time of the Pharaohs in Egypt. These beliefs are centered on a deep spirituality, believing in both ghosts and in a type of magic cast by charms, potions and amulets.

⟨⟩Casting Roots & Boo Hags⟨⟩

This magical ability to cast spells is called 'conjuring', or 'casting roots'. The pronunciations of these are, respectively, "con-juh-ing" and "casting ruts". A magic spell itself is called a 'conjure'. The spell is often cast by burying a bag or bundle on the property of the unsuspecting victim. There are also ways of conjuring involving secret potions to drink, powders, nail clippings, and that most powerful of talismans—graveyard dirt. Someone skilled in the art of casting spells is called a root doctor, or a witch doctor. They can be employed if you feel that magic is being used against you, and for a fee they will protect you from evil.

Different from a witch doctor is a witch themselves, often called a 'boo-hag' or simply a 'hag'. Not to be confused with the Hollywood version, witches in this tradition look no different than regular people. Witches are more akin to modern-day vampires, because the belief is that they not only suck blood, but also steal the life-force or essence of the victim. To have your essence or blood stolen by a witch is known as 'being rid' or 'ridden'. If someone looks poor or sickly, the assumption is that a hag stole that person's energy in the middle of the night; they are being "rid by a witch."

One example of this took place in the 1940's. On the eastern edge of town there is an area that used to be called Old Fort. A man named Jack Wilson had married a girl named Evie, even though another woman, Malinda, had shown a lot of interest in being his bride. A few months into the marriage, Jack and his new bride were beginning to feel weak and tired. Jack noticed that he would feel more tired upon waking than he had when he went to bed, so he began to suspect that he was the target of being rid by a witch. He didn't tell Evie what he suspected, deciding instead to lay a trap. He went to bed at the usual time, but he only pretended to sleep. He had taken to bed with him a large axe-handle, which he put alongside himself under the covers. His wife dozed off, and for a long while nothing happened. Just as Jack himself had started to fall asleep, he heard the window in the bedroom sliding open. He could hear someone or some*thing* enter the room. Jack remained motionless and waited. He felt something on the bed, so he opened his eyes and saw a large black cat on the bed between him and his sleeping wife. It climbed onto Evie, and she began to cough and choke in her sleep.

That is when Jack decided to jump out of bed and swing the axe handle at the cat. He hit it in the side and it screamed with rage—but it was a woman's scream it let out! The cat scrambled off the bed and leapt out of the window into the night. Jack ran to his wife to help her.

The next morning, Jack put his hunting dog on the scent of the cat. He took the axe handle along, too. The dog followed the trail about half a mile, stopping at some bushes. The dog began to snarl and bark. Jack pushed the bushes aside and found Malinda. She was lying on her side, with three broken ribs. When she saw he still had the axe handle in his hand, Malinda begged Jack: "Please don't hit me again, I promise to leave you and Evie alone!"

৵ৎ Haint Blue ৵ৎ

Another Geechee tradition is the color of Haint Blue, a color that is supposed to repel evil spirits. This color is interpreted as a 'sky blue color,' or even as deep as a medium Cerulean blue. As detailed in the sections devoted to the Hampton Lillibridge House and Owens-Thomas House, the color symbolizes water in the Geechee culture, because water is seen as a protector in that tradition. It is believed that an evil spirit will not cross water to harm you—and this idea of water as talisman from evil spirits is not limited to this belief system. In our own Western culture, baptism is symbolically seen to wash away sins, Holy water repels vampires, and even in Hollywood, the Wicked Witch of the West was melted away by that very universal solvent!

The paint was made with a mixture of indigo dye, milk, and lime. It was painted many places for protection of the family within: under the overhang of front porches, around windows and doors, on window shutters, or even underneath the chairs inside the home. This idea of 'haint' blue as a protector may have had a practical value, because the lime would act as a natural insect repellent. Since mosquitoes were the transmitter of Yellow Fever, the Geechee may have stumbled unwittingly into a practice of shielding themselves from one of the most feared diseases of the 19th century.

The more one walks through the Historic District and in parts of the Victorian area of town, the more one cannot help but notice the haint blue color up underneath front porch overhangs and around the windows of the homes. This is still very much a tradition in this unique Southern city, regardless of whether the inhabitant of the house in question is still, or was ever, associated with Geechee culture. Even young trendy couples seeking to capture some old-world authenticity to their historic home have been known to paint haint blue around their homes—perhaps even unaware of the deep spiritual meaning of the color they chose with such triteness.

৵ৎ First African Baptist Church ৵ৎ

The First African Baptist Church on Franklin Square is the oldest black congregation in America, with the first service being held in 1788. The current structure was built in 1859. Among the church's features are beautiful stained glass windows, and a decorative carving on the floor, which actually housed a deep and guarded secret.

Hidden under the floor is a secret passage, which was one stop along the path of the so-called 'Underground Railroad', a series of safe-houses for escaped slaves fleeing Northward before and during the Civil War. The intricate carving served as air holes when these runaway slaves were being hidden underneath to avoid re-capture.

↝Kevin Barry's Irish Pub↜

The abominable slave practice espoused first by England, and then the United States, has repercussions even today, and evidence of this foul traffic of human lives still exists in our present-day city. Many people living and working in structures built with Savannah Grey bricks are unaware that these building blocks of the Historic District were fashioned by hands bound in chains. The Hermitage Plantation, located right outside of Savannah and owned by Henry McAlpin, was responsible chiefly for the production of Savannah Grey bricks, and their output was largely accomplished by slaves. But these are not the only evidence of this despicable custom, as shown in the section entitled *B. Matthews Eatery.*

Another clue to our ties with slavery is at Kevin Barry's Irish Pub, located on River Street. This pub and restaurant is a former warehouse, and there are sections of the structure which date as far back as 1814. Part of the bottom floor is built out of ballast stones, brought over in the holds of ships bound from ports all over the world. Along with the best Irish stew in Savannah, the old building also has past associations with human chattel.

Located on the back wall of the far east room there are a series of bolts in the wall, along with holes drilled into the very rock comprising the ballast stone wall. These bolts were once linked to chains binding slaves to the walls of the old structure. Even though the slave trade had technically been outlawed by 1798 in Georgia and nationally by 1808, slave traders still had free reign importing Negroes because of a disinterested legislature and indifferent inspectors.

One other sign points to illicit slaves being housed in this location: a bit of graffiti carved into the ballast stone construction. As one enters Kevin Barry's on the ground floor entrance, one can view a large black stone making up part of the wall directly to the right of the door, under the lamp. One may need a lighter or a match to illuminate the carving for a proper viewing, but the sketch is truly worth the effort. The profile of a man is clearly visible, and he is wearing what appears to be either a wig or skullcap. According to the owner, Vic Powers, this is possibly a caricature of the slaver, or perhaps even the likeness of an already-purchased slave's master. The handiwork of the image is quite good; although the artisan is untrained, the representation is undeniable.

One wonders at the thought process of the artist as he made this image so long ago. An uncertain fate clearly awaited him or her—was this an attempt at levity, or was there a more serious purpose in mind? Was the sketch completed? This is yet one more unexplained story in this, our wondrous yet strange Southern city.

✑Slave Ship 'Wanderer'✑

In 1858, a group of men headed by Savannah planter Charles Lamar defied the U.S. government and set into motion one of the most controversial and politically charged court cases in American history. Many believe that the fallout from the actions of that reckless and headstrong group may have hastened the country's plunge into bloody Civil War. Their crime? Lamar and his band of outlaw businessmen trafficked human cargo, and thus violated both the 1798 Georgia law and 1808 federal law banning the importation of slaves, with the voyage of the slave ship Wanderer.

Reckless and headstrong: two words that describe Charles Augustus Lafayette Lamar. His fiery red hair was matched only by his temper. Charles was held during his baptism by his godfather, Revolutionary War hero Marquis de Lafayette, but unfortunately the only part of Lafayette which rubbed off on Lamar was his name.

Lamar was already considered the wealthiest man in Savannah, but he became obsessed with restarting the slave trade, in spite of the laws against it. Lamar's own family got wind of his plans and attempted to talk him out of the scheme. In a letter to his father he arrogantly wondered: what the difference was between going to Virginia or Africa to buy a slave? His father wrote back: "An expedition to the moon would have been equally sensible, and no more contrary to the laws of Providence. May God forgive you for all your attempts to violate his will and his laws." But Lamar was undeterred.

In 1857, Lamar tried to buy a ship, the *E. A. Rawling*, in order to make his scheme a reality, but the federal government seized it under suspicion that it was being converted to a 'slaver'. Charles, along with three businessmen, finally bought the Wanderer, a sleek and swift sailing vessel designed for racing. The craft was built in Long Island, and after the sale made port in Brunswick, Georgia, some sixty miles south of Savannah. After a short stay, it left port, bound for the shores of Africa.

Upon arriving in the Congo, the crew reached a deal to buy between 600 and 750 men between the ages of thirteen and eighteen at a cost of between one and three dollars a head. These men had been captured by rival tribes—kidnapped for the very purpose of being sold into slavery. The ship by this time had been outfitted with special cargo holds to hold human captives. On her return voyage, the speedy craft eluded both the English and American navies, and slipped past the U.S. fortification guarding the approach to Brunswick. Lamar himself, it is said, distracted the officers of the fort by throwing a lavish party.

On the open market these same slaves which had sold in the Congo for three dollars each now fetched a price of between five and seven hundred dollars, an obscene profit for Lamar and his trio of investors. But greed was their driving force, and they tried their luck again at another run, hoping for similar results. It was not to be.

Everything started smoothly. The speedy ship once again evaded the authorities, the sale of the captives in the Congo went without incident, and the swift craft encountered no difficulties getting back to the United States. Lamar even allegedly threw another party, distracting the authorities.

But here is where the whole scheme went awry. The ship made port at a plantation on Jekyll Island, Georgia. In a stormy sea, the cargo of just over four hundred freshly-imported slaves were unloaded. The storm was a portent of things to come, because immediately the rumors began to circulate about the Wanderer's illicit runs to the Congo. The federal government got involved and began looking for evidence, including the contraband human cargo. Even President James Buchanan got involved—he was petitioned by the U.S. Senate to investigate the shady dealings of one Charles Lamar and the Wanderer. The ship was impounded by U.S. Marshals. The Georgia man who had piloted the craft to Jekyll Island for an outrageous fee decided to turn down Lamar's bribe and testify in the mounting case against the Wanderer investors. The developments drew worldwide attention, and several Northern papers wrote scathing editorials condemning Lamar and the actions of his investors. But the case quickly resembled a farce.

Lamar and his associates scrambled to hide the evidence, including the new slaves. Prosecutors found that Lamar and his band of investors had been very clever in covering their tracks, and whatever evidence once linked Lamar to the ship no longer existed. Even the slaves had disappeared. The case against Lamar was largely circumstantial. The sentence handed down by Judge Moore Wayne seems equally farcical: a five hundred dollar fine, and thirty days in jail, which Lamar and his associates were allowed to serve in Lamar's apartments located above his office.

The Wanderer was sold at public auction at the U.S. Customs House on Bay Street. The winning bidder's name? Charles Augustus Lafayette Lamar. There was talk that Lamar bullied and threatened the other bidders for the Wanderer to keep the price low. This seems confirmed by the fact that Lamar knocked down a man who had dared bid against him. The winning bidder also resented the editorials written by the Northern papers, and the hot-blooded Lamar even challenged Horace Greeley of the New York Tribune to a duel, which Greeley wisely ignored.

Lamar had plans of making other illicit runs with the Wanderer, but events in the Civil War intervened. The ship was seized once again by the North, who ironically enough turned it into part of the blockade of Southern ports. The Wanderer was eventually sold at auction once again after the war, and became a commercial vessel. She foundered off the coast of Cuba, running aground. The hulk was visible on the beach for many years until time and tide reduced her to nothingness.

Charles Lamar did not outlive the ship which will forever be associated with his name. He joined the Confederacy and died on Easter Sunday, 1865, defending Columbus, Georgia. He is buried in Laurel Grove Cemetery. Inscribed on his monument are the words:

"In the morning it flourisheth and groweth up; in the evening it is cut down and withereth."

Perhaps there is a double meaning in the verse: Lamar's life, and also the abominable practice of slavery.

ᴄᴏA Modern-Day Wanderer ᴄᴏ

There is one last Savannah connection: for years, the St. Patrick's Day celebration had a float in the form of a pirate ship. It featured a man in a gorilla costume in chains. From time to time, the gorilla would break the bonds and 'escape' into the crowd and grab children. Most in the crowd considered it harmless fun. But in 1999, a professor visiting the festivities from out of town noticed that the ship was named the 'Wanderer'. The horrible connotation left many in Savannah embarrassed at the unintentional bad taste, and the new 'Wanderer' was dry-docked—for good.

More Savannah Hauntings

The same ignorance makes me so bold as to deny absolutely the truth of the various ghost stories, and yet with the common, though strange, reservation that while I doubt any one of them, I still have faith in the whole of them taken together.

—Immanuel Kant
Dreams of a Spirit-Seer

Living in Historic downtown Savannah means hearing lots of ghost stories from locals. Naysayers might invoke the old saying: Savannah is bisected by Bull Street, so we Savannahians naturally have a line of 'Bull' down our center. But to be a native of Savannah is to accept the strange supernatural flair of this city. You don't find many atheists in foxholes, to be sure, and you don't find many skeptics in Savannah. The cynical words of those who would disparage this city's haunted reputation are crushed under the weight of so many unsolicited stories.

These stories are sometimes related to me in passing, but I feel that when taken all together, these begin to paint an accurate portrait of why Savannah is considered to be a truly unique place to live. I have culled the best from these separate tales into one chapter.

∽Laurel Grove Cemetery∽

On the southwestern side of Savannah, just outside of the Historic District, there exists a beautiful burial ground worthy of Savannah royalty. Included in the esteemed roll call of the interments here are Juliette Gordon Low, founder of the Girl Scouts, 'Waving Girl' Florence Martus, James Pierpont, composer of Jingle Bells, and a host of Confederate dead, including Francis Bartow and Gilbert Moxley Sorrel.

Laurel Grove Cemetery was established in 1852, as a partial answer to the rampant overcrowded conditions at Colonial Park Cemetery. The authorities actually invited all citizens with loved ones buried in Colonial Park could re-inter them in Laurel Grove, free of charge, and between 1852 and 1888 close to six hundred were relocated. The resulting cemetery was massive—a testament to the hard conditions during the 19th century.

I found myself in this enchanting cemetery at the personal invitation of Colin Young, preeminent historian and authority on everything having to do with Laurel Grove. Colin, a native of Atlanta, had heard of my efforts to compile a book of Savannah ghost stories, and he graciously took several hours out of his day walking me around on a personal tour. I found it hard to keep up: physically, mentally and intellectually.

When asked if Laurel Grove had any ghost stories, Colin's eyes twinkled. "Oh yes, sir," he said, and began walking at his brisk pace yet again. "Several. I'll show you." We approached a small, relatively well-cared for lot. It was here that Colin related a story about a sighting of a man in period attire. "It is important that you not reveal the lot number," Colin warned, "This is a cemetery, not a tourist attraction. There are those who would visit after reading the account and try to take souvenirs. That is something we have had problems with out here in the past."

"Two workers were restoring this lot. One was a believer in ghosts, the other not. As they worked, the one non-believer spotted something out of the ordinary. He claims that he saw a man in 19th century

clothing standing in a lot very near them, and that the man was as real as you or I. He turned and asked his co-worker, 'Who's that in the lot over there?' When he turned back, the man had gone... vanished into thin air."

Colin had brought along several instruments, including a magnetometer, which measures electromagnetic fluctuations. He and I did record some strange fluctuations in the area, but Colin said with apparent dissatisfaction, "It is usually much more active than this. My friend and I encountered an anomaly out here which was three feet in circumference, and was cylindrical. The odd readings started at ground level and went as high as we could measure."

There was also a storage shed which Colin pointed out as the site of some strange happenings. "We had stowed a ladder up above a compartment, packing it away very securely. As we left, the ladder somehow worked its way loose and flung itself to the ground inside the shed. We all heard it hit the ground with a surprising degree of force."

And so among the impressive list of the dead at Laurel Grove Cemetery, there are those whom eternal rest proves elusive.

⚐Drive-By Haunting⚐

A man named Mike who works at a local hospital told me the following tale over drinks one night. He said that early one evening as he was driving home from a meeting, he saw something that he cannot explain. As he was heading up Price Street, which is a one way street which heads south, he passed what can only be called an apparition. "I was driving on Price, and saw something unusual," he explained. "I saw a girl standing at the corner of State Street with a dog, but the girl was in period costume. I'm no expert with time periods or costumes, but she didn't look like she was from the Civil War—it looked older than that." Mike then added, "I wondered if she was part of a reenactment, and I also worried that her dog wasn't on a leash, and she was close to traffic. I looked in the rearview mirror to get a better look, and she had vanished. We're talking about a period of seconds here; there was no way she could have disappeared that quickly. But she did. I nearly wrecked my car."

⚐Ghosts at Garibaldi's?⚐

A former server at the upscale restaurant Garibaldi's, located on West Congress Street, related the following story:

She worked at the restaurant for a number of months while the building was being renovated. The eatery was being expanded into the upstairs, and was getting a facelift downstairs as well. When she started the job, the servers described often hearing footsteps above them on the still-in-progress second floor renovation. When they would investigate, the upper floor would be deserted. She didn't particularly believe her fellow workers, suspecting them of having a laugh at her expense.

Then, early one evening, she heard footsteps above her on the second floor. Thinking it might be one of the managers, and needing a question answered, she stepped into the upstairs before she began her shift. But she found herself in a deserted room. Hearing disembodied footsteps turned into a common occurrence for her during her employment as a waitress at Garibaldi's.

Another blustery January evening, she and a friend were having a drink at the Rail, which is a bar a couple of blocks away on Congress Street. On their way home they decided to walk over to Garibaldi's to see if their co-worker was finished with her shift. Peering through the glass, they glimpsed a woman from behind walking down the downstairs hallway. Thinking this was their friend, they tapped loudly on the glass to catch her attention, but she continued walking away from them without looking back, and disappeared into the gloom of the hallway. Thinking that their friend has simply not heard them, they decided to call her cell phone. The friend answered immediately—and informed them that she was already home. The restaurant had been slow and they had closed early. Garibaldi's was deserted—at least by the living.

The Planters Inn Apparition

The Planters Inn on Reynolds Square is also reputed to be haunted. The ghost apparently has a bit of Obsessive-Compulsive Disorder, because this female spirit is said to straighten picture frames that are off-kilter.

This picture-straightening phantasm has been seen in the rooms, in the hallways, and even was seen one night in the lobby by several eyewitnesses simultaneously. She has been reported to appear, level the offending picture, and then disappear.

No one knows the identity of this apparition, but the Empire-waisted nightgown she is said to wear gives a few clues as to her profession. The Planters Inn used to be called the John Wesley Hotel, and for a time in Savannah had the reputation of most upscale brothel in town. Indeed, historian Rebecca Clark related a story involving a downstairs beauty salon where her mother forbid her to visit the

Wesley Hotel—the owner, Mr. Davis, had to visit the Clark home to do Rebecca's hair, instead. "Nice girls did *not* frequent that hotel," Becky said with a smile.

☜The Olde Harbour Inn☞

Situated on the east end of River Street, the Olde Harbor Inn overlooks the Savannah River, its exterior largely unchanged from the 19th century. The stone foundation of Olde Harbour Inn was laid nearly 200 years ago, but in 1892, a swift blaze caused nearly complete destruction of the original building. The current structure was then rebuilt on the ballast stone foundation. The building was the former home to Standard Oil Company until 1907. In 1930, it was occupied by Alexander Brothers Company, a blue jeans and overall factory. The entire building was renovated in 1985, and was opened as the Olde Harbour Inn in 1987.

It has been said that during this 1892 fire that a surly worker named Hank lost his life. Many suspect Hank of setting the blaze himself, because the flames began around his office, and he was in an argument with management at the time of the suspicious incident. If he did indeed set the blaze, then Hank's revenge backfired, because he lost his life in the inferno. He was the fire's only fatality.

Hank still has a reputation of being surly. He has been known to knock on doors, twist door knobs, and even more disturbingly, he's been known to stretch out across the bed with unsuspecting guests. One woman awakened one night to feel the mattress compressing next to her. Thinking it was her husband, she rolled away and attempted to go back to sleep. Only then did she see her husband sleepily walk out of the bathroom door towards the bed. The 'someone' on the bed with her was not her husband! She screamed and rolled out of bed.

Apparently (and unfortunately for that couple), being the grouchiest ghost in Savannah can sometimes get pretty lonely.

☜Spirit at Ft. Jackson☞

According to the Travel Channel program 'America's Most Haunted Places-Savannah', old Fort Jackson situated just east of Savannah on the river has some surprising supernatural stories.

Begun in 1808 because of worsening relations with Britain, the brick stronghold was still in use during the time of the Civil War. It became a Confederate fortification, protecting Savannah from a sea-borne Union invasion. And it was during this time that a Rebel soldier set in motion an event which still has psychic repercussions at the fort: he attempted to murder his superior officer.

No one is quite sure the exact circumstances involved in the incident between Private Patrick Garrity and Lieutenant George Dickerson. What we do know is that Private Garrity was on guard duty near the drawbridge, and was approached by Lt. Dickerson. Garrity, for reasons unknown, bludgeoned his superior with his musket, breaking both his musket and the officer's skull in four places. Private Garrity then attempted to evade his pursuers by jumping into the moat, where he then drowned. The Lieutenant survived his beating, but never fully recovered. He was unable remember the incident, much less give a reason for the attack.

There has been an apparition seen at the spot of the attack, and most assume it is the ghost of Garrity. The site manager one night was closing the fort, and saw a silhouette on the parade ground of the fort of a Confederate soldier walking alone in a long grey frock coat. The apparition was only visible from the waist up. The site manager calmly recorded the incident in the daily log book, and then left for the evening.

Another silhouette of a soldier has been reported standing on the casement walls above the parade ground by both the site manager and by several other eyewitnesses.

There has also been an incident involving an award given out every year to reenactors stationed at Ft. Jackson. On numerous occasions, the award has broken or has parts turn up missing right in the area that Garrity attacked his superior, then drowned.

Is this a case of Garrity still taking out his aggressions on fellow soldiers? Or is his frustration that his side of the story is yet untold? Perhaps for Private Garrity to finally rest in the afterlife, these questions must be answered, and he can find the peace that eluded him in life.

❦Frightful Presence on Liberty Street❧

This story comes from a relative of the young family in question. It seems a family moved south into a rented West Liberty Street dwelling. But the trio was quickly found not to suit their new house, instead of the other way around. The family began to have unexplainable incidents, such as hearing strange footsteps and catching fleeting glimpses of something (or someone) out of the corners of their eyes.

The mother of the family especially began to take issue with the fact that she kept hearing someone walking down the hallway in the upstairs and closing the door behind them, and occasionally the door would be found closed when they were expressly leaving the door open for their daughter, who was still being potty-trained. She would always notice this in the late evenings—and would get up to check on what she assumed was her daughter using the rest room and would find no one there. Sometimes the young mother would find pills which had been taken down from the cabinet sitting beside the sink—and she even scolded her little girl, who claimed that she hadn't touched them. The little girl would also talk frequently about being visited in the night by an older woman, but the mother assumed it was just the girl's way of missing her grandmother, whom they had moved several hours away from when they moved from Atlanta.

Finally the couple and their young girl got settled, more or less, in their new home. They decided to entertain some guests at a dinner party, which they figured would be a great way to meet the neighbors. As they were serving dinner, one of their new neighbors, an elderly woman, sat staring at them with a very disturbed expression on her face. Finally she stammered an excuse and left rather abruptly.

The elderly woman called the next day to apologize for her bizarre and un-neighborly behavior the previous evening. She then went on to explain her strange actions: she revealed that the woman that lived in the house years before, a thoroughly dour and unpleasant woman named Dottie, became even more so when her husband died. She finally took her own life.

"I've always had what some people call 'second sight'," the neighbor revealed, "I've never been quite sure if it was a curse or a blessing. All that I *am* sure of is that I left your party last night because suddenly *I could see Dottie following you around last night as you were preparing the meal!*" She went on to say that she could only see her from the waist up, and the rest was just a blur, or as if the woman's legs were made of gauze. Unable to say what she (and she alone) could see in mixed company, the neighbor simply fled the party.

The young mother asked through stiff lips, "Where did Dottie die?" But she already knew the answer: "Why, she died in the upstairs bathroom, dear. She took pills and ended her own life."

The young family moved out of their unwelcoming dwelling in record time. Happily, their new apartment held no such unpleasant surprises.

Phantom on Congress Street

Kevin, a bartender at McDonough's Restaurant and Lounge admits that he is a skeptic in the true sense when it comes to ghosts. "I don't believe, and I don't disbelieve. I've never had any kind of experience with that stuff." His longtime girlfriend is another matter. One night while Kevin was at work, she was relaxing on the couch with her cat at their apartment, located above the Savannah Bistro on Congress Street.

She suddenly saw an apparition walk through the dining room. This indistinct apparition walked into another room, paused near the fireplace, and then vanished. As she sat there blinking, wondering if she had really seen what she thought she had, she realized that the cat had clearly seen something, as well. All of the cat's fur was standing on end, and it was looking intently in the direction of the now-vanished spectre.

Haunted Orphanage on Houston Street

Savannah is a town of tragedy, and life in Colonial Georgia was incredibly hard. So many died in the early years of the city that there arose a need to care for those orphaned by disease and fire. The oldest orphanage in America, Bethesda, was located right outside of Savannah. So many unfortunate children were placed at Bethesda that it grew too large and was divided in half in the early 1800's: one half for boys, the other for girls. The 1810 structure located at 117 Houston Street housed the girl's section of the orphanage.

Sadly, the tragedy visited on all these orphan girls did not end with the death of their parents. This structure burned shortly after the orphans were moved in, starting in the lower-level kitchen. Most of the girls escaped the fire, but some were trapped upstairs. It is said that two of the little girls that died were sisters who had only arrived at the orphanage that day, not long enough for anyone to even learn their names. They were found hugging each other tightly even in death. All that anyone ever remembered about them was that they both had long blonde hair.

It is perhaps this tragic end that has bound these sisters' life force energy to the former orphanage. The energy released in the fire, the special bond between sisters, and the fateful way they met their death have seemingly combined to make a powerful connection to this area—both the former orphanage and the square itself. Not only have the girls been seen inside the home numerous times, but also playing out in Greene Square. Concerned neighbors have called the police, thinking that these two little girls were being left unattended by careless parents, but when police arrived to investigate, the girls had vanished.

ఆThe Earl Grey Ghostఴ

In a 1924 yellow brick condominium-style apartment building, there are reports of a ghost with some baggage: *tea* bags, to be precise.

It seems a young couple moved into their new apartment, located at the corner of Abercorn and State Streets on Oglethorpe Square. They loved everything about their new place except for one thing: a strange recurrence in the kitchen. Often times upon awaking, they would find teacups sitting out, as if they had just missed someone sitting at their kitchen counter. "Sometimes, it would be just the empty cup sitting on an empty saucer, but on occasion we would find the actual remains of a cup of tea, with teabag, in the bottom of the cup," the young lady related. "Now, neither my boyfriend nor I drink hot tea, which is the funny part. I'm from the South, so for me it's sweet tea or nothing. He's even English, and that's sort of our joke, the fact that I fell in love with the one Englishman who doesn't like hot tea!"

The young lady began to get nervous, because someone was obviously using their kitchen without their consent. "I was hoping that there was an innocent explanation, like a neighbor who had a key or something. But of course your mind starts to envision the 'Tea-Drinking Slasher', that sort of thing. We even changed the locks in the apartment, but it continued—I'd say once a week or so, we'd find a teacup."

Finally, exasperated, they called the former owner, a young man named Rodney. His answer surprised the couple, because he related the following story:

Rodney had been forced to sell his former apartment because his girlfriend wouldn't come anywhere near the place after an incident in the kitchen. She had stayed over the previous night, and got up early the next morning for a bit of coffee. It was there that she unexpectedly ran face-to face with Rodney's mother, who was sitting at the kitchen table, drinking a cup of hot tea and wearing a yellow bathrobe. She was mortified, because she hadn't even known Rodney's mother was in town visiting—the two had never even met, and the setting for their first meeting were less than ideal, you might say. After exchanging pleasantries, she slipped back to the bedroom and woke Rodney up, and began to chastise him for not warning her that his mother was in town. Rodney looked at her very strangely, and then calmly informed her that his mother had died two years previous. She was visiting Rodney and the then-new apartment, and suffered a massive stroke, and died. *When Rodney's mother died, she had been sitting at the kitchen table, wearing a yellow bathrobe and drinking her customary cup of hot tea.*

The new young couple was faced with a terrible choice: sell their lovely new apartment, or live with the knowledge that they were in a supernatural time-share situation with Rodney's dead mother. They wound up compromising. "We left Rodney's dead mom a note," the young lady explained, "We wrote her a nice letter, explaining that Rodney had moved. After that evening it was the last time we had a problem with the teacups, so apparently she got the message."

With a mischievous wink, the girl added, "We even gave her Rodney's new address, in case she wanted to visit."

᪥Ghosts and Real Estate᪥

Nicole Hubbard, a friend of this author and former owner of a tour company, told the following story one day about her experience while looking for a house. She and her first husband, Jason, had arranged to look at a piece of property near the corner of Broughton and Price Streets, and were met there by the realtor. While they were inside, Jason went upstairs while she stayed downstairs speaking to the realtor, Jeff, about the property.

Suddenly, Jason came back downstairs, looking very strange. "Jason was an ex-Army Ranger, a pretty tough guy. He wasn't scared of much, but he looked scared," Nicole related. "He asked the realtor whether the place was haunted. Well, the realtor got a sheepish look on his face and confirmed that yes, the place had previously had reports—and even Jeff himself had experienced a few instances when he had lived there.

"Jeff and his wife kept hearing a baby crying in the upstairs, and thinking it was their child, would rush upstairs to see what was wrong, only to find their child sleeping peacefully. This apparently happened over and over."

Nicole smiled as she told the following part of the story: "Needless to say, there was no sale. Once we were outside, Jason told me that he had felt such a feeling of dread on the upper floor that he had to get out. He said it felt like there was something evil on the second floor of that house. Of course, perhaps the spirit was reacting to him... my first husband was a pretty strange fellow, that's all I'll say. Maybe the ghost wanted nothing to do with him."

To this author, though, the ghost story is not the most unusual part of the tale. It is the honest realtor!

᪥Oglethorpe House᪥

One of Savannah College of Art & Design's main downtown dormitories is Oglethorpe House, which is affectionately called 'O-House' by the students housed there. Built in the late 1950's, this six-story modern-style building was originally a hotel, called the Downtowner Motor Lodge. It became a Ramada Inn during its history, and was eventually sold to Savannah College of Art & Design for use as a dorm. So now the dorm is 'haunted', if you'll pardon the expression, by a group of pierced and tattooed SCAD students.

Many supernatural stories persist about the structure. Separating the folklore and myths from the real stories is difficult work—any time you have a group of young, impressionable, and creative people all living in a confined space, you will hear tall tales. Sometimes, too, the stories are fueled by more than caffeine and an over-active imagination. Dismissing the easily distinguishable urban legends (any tale involving deranged killers, messages written in blood or the like are standard fare), several stories told about the space have the ring of truth.

One such tale involves the Emerald Room across the street. When Savannah entered her great decline in the 1960's, bars such as the Emerald Room were inevitable. Several ladies of ill repute would ply their trade at the bar, and the convenient proximity of the Downtowner Motor Lodge made it a prime spot for business to be conducted. One of these ladies of the night met an awful fate at the hands of a client on the fifth floor. It has been said that her heels can still be heard clicking on the walkways even today, when no one is visible.

One young lady insists that it isn't high heels she hears clicking, but marbles. She and her roommate have heard marbles being dropped and rolling outside her room on numerous occasions. Her room is located on the top floor of Oglethorpe House, so the sound definitely has to be coming from right outside their room, but nevertheless they find no one outside and nothing amiss. The legend, unverifiable but persistent, concerns a young boy who died in the old hotel while playing with marbles. Perhaps then, if the stories are true, his spirit still plays in the old hallways.

Conservative Savannahians, viewing the blue hair and multiple piercings, often say that SCAD students have lost their marbles—but this is one case where the marbles were lost long before SCAD was on the scene.

M ore Strange Savannah Stories

"That spot of spots! That place of places! That city of cities!"

-2nd Lieutenant Robert E. Lee,
referring to Savannah

"Savannah in the province of Georgia remains the death trap of human society."

-Hessian commander Colonel von Porbeck

Ah, Savannah! A contradiction at every turn, yet we love her. The incongruity of the above quotes could almost sum up this unique Lowcountry jewel. With each strange non sequitur, she becomes even more attractive—one must simply accept the contradictions to understand her... all that is required is to shake your head and mutter, "Only in Savannah." Sayings abound about this city: it has been said that you are not a true Savannahian until your first name and your last name are the same. For an answer to that question, I suppose we'd have to ask Sheftall Sheftall or Minis Minis about the veracity of the saying.

Savannah is an odd town; there is no sugar-coating that fact. This inherent abnormality certainly generates some great tales. Georgia's First City just seems to be brimming with bizarre, amusing, or scarcely believable stories. From the very beginning of her history, she began to generate some legendary goings-on. For instance, there were four things prohibited in the new colony: no lawyers, no slavery, no Catholic services, and no strong spirits, rum or brandy. It was therefore an embarrassment to all when one of the colonists immediately got into trouble with strong drink in the Indian camp, and had to be escorted back to Savannah by force.

In fact, Savannah has been known for having an abundance of these four prohibitions at various times during her history.

Savannahians have made pushing the edge of the envelope a defining trait—making us a colorful lot. Without further ado, here is a small selected sampling of my favorite small stories.

౿ᷯᴖMagistrate for a Night⸱ᷧᴖ

In the early days of Savannah, we didn't have a governor because we were not a Royal Province. Instead, we were overseen by the Trustees, who appointed Magistrates, a title whose power rested roughly between being mayor and a modern state Governor.

One of our earliest Magistrates was Henry Parker, who had quite a taste for rum. This was unfortunate for Henry, because rum was forbidden in Savannah. In 1739, Henry staggered into Jenkins' Tavern, already having knocked back a considerable amount of the hard liquor. Henry was out of money, so in order to quench his thirst that night he offered the owner of the tavern, Edward Jenkins, a deal. In exchange for a whole bowl of rum punch, they would trade places and jobs for the night: barkeep would become Magistrate, and vice versa. The barkeeper considered this for a moment, and then accepted the offer. The two even traded clothes to make the deal even more official.

The new Magistrate stepped out from behind the bar, and the new tavern keeper stepped behind and began to serve drinks. When Henry asked for the bowl of rum punch he was promised, the new Magistrate Jenkins exercised his new authority: he called Henry a 'drunken swab' and grabbed him by the scruff of the neck. He then chastised him for debasing the office of Magistrate, and threw him to the floor. The bartender-for-a-night never did get his bowl of punch, because rum was strictly forbidden in Savannah.

Henry Parker had been a linen draper back in London, so perhaps it could be said that he made a career out of being three sheets to the wind.

౿ᷯᴖSecret Tunnels⸱ᷧᴖ

There are other tunnels in Savannah, in addition to the ones already detailed in this volume (see chapters entitled 'Pirate's House' and 'B. Matthews Bakery & Eatery'). The briefly earlier-referenced tunnel (in the chapter on 'Old Cemeteries') at Candler Hospital was supposedly used to smuggle Yellow Fever epidemic victims out across Drayton Street into an unknown terminus in Forsyth Park. This was done to prevent the populace from panicking, since the authorities were wishing to keep secret how many fatalities were being caused by the dreaded killer Yellow Fever. Historians disagree on the veracity of the story, but the tunnel undoubtedly exists. Inside Candler Hospital is the long-since bricked-up entrance to the old tunnel. There are stories circulating involving secret autopsies occurring in the passageway, and there is talk that the area served as a makeshift morgue.

Another strange tunnel without easy explanation comes from an undated handwritten letter found in the Georgia Historical Society archives. A property owner on Liberty Street between Bull and Drayton Streets encountered two men digging on his property in the alleyway behind his house. When he confronted them, they claimed to have both a permit to dig and permission from the owner—which was impossible, since he was the actual owner of the property. He called the police, but the men both fled. Police investigated the hole the two had been excavating, and found the remains of a tunnel entrance where no known passage was supposed to exist. The officer peered each way down the old brick tunnel with a flashlight, and clambered out of the hole, suddenly deciding that the passage should be sealed up. The hole was buried, and the property owner was instructed to leave the site alone, without any explanation for what they had found or what the tunnel's purpose could be.

Were these men simple thieves, or treasure hunters? And who originally constructed the underground passage, and why? Was this a smuggler's haven? Or some legitimate passageway whose purpose is now unknown? These questions remain unanswered even today, and short of getting permission from the current owner and from the city and starting an excavation, unanswered will they remain.

☞Historic Firefighters or a Burning Lie?☜

Savannah firefighters are many things: brave, hard-working, and if my female friends are to be believed, they are also very attractive. But the one thing they are not: reliable sources of history for unsuspecting tourists. The firefighters often sit out on the benches at night next to the downtown firehouse at the corner of Abercorn Street and Oglethorpe Avenue. This is incidentally across the street from the front gates of Colonial Park Cemetery, which is where our nightly walking tour, The Savannah Haunted History Tour, begins, so we tour guides have frequent contact with the firefighters, often with hilarious results.

One night I was walking back to the corner to begin my second tour of the evening when I overheard a conversation between a tourist and these fellows on the corner. The woman asked if the cemetery was the one featured in the book *Midnight and the Garden of Good and Evil* (it isn't—that honor belongs to Bonaventure Cemetery a few miles to the east). Apparently this particular fireman had been asked that question a few too many times, because he informed her that yes, it was in fact where they had filmed that particular sequence. Assuming this was a rookie who was giving out mistaken trivia, I started to interrupt, but this fellow continued his spiel. He told her that what she was looking at was in reality a Hollywood movie prop put up by the studio, and that all the gravestones and burial vaults were made out of fiberglass because "the real cemetery burned down twenty years ago."

I was stunned into silence, fully expecting this woman to catch on to his obvious joke. I mean, how exactly does a cemetery burn down? And even if that were possible it would still be unlikely since it is located across the street from a firehouse. But the woman nodded and exclaimed that the movie people had done an excellent job recreating the cemetery, and it wasn't it nice that the city had left it up for the tourists?

The moral of the story? Just because someone wears an official-looking outfit does not make them above trickery on those unsuspecting. This gives new meaning to 'liar, liar, pants on fire'.

I myself ran afoul of the firefighters' trickery one night: just to amuse themselves they hid an electronic noisemaker in the bushes near the cemetery gates. There is no polite way to describe the sounds that this remote-controlled noisemaker produced, so let me just say that there are obvious jokes involving tour guides being full of hot air. As I began my introduction, completely unawares, the firefighters struck with their joke: my sentences were punctuated with different types of audible gastric movements worthy of a wild boar, perhaps, or an elephant stricken with indigestion. I had no choice but to continue, and judging from the reaction of the crowd, they had assumed that these rumblings were coming from *me,* and several even took a step back. My face matched the fire truck across the way by the end of my introduction.

I did, however, exact some measure of revenge. The firefighters left their electronic prank in the same location for my second tour of the evening—a huge tactical error. I quickly found the offending device in the grass near the gate, and in full view of the peanut gallery on the benches across the street, filled it full of the ice water I carry with me in my haversack. It seems the intestinal rumblings from the machine were quickly calmed by the water, because it never uttered another sound.

ᴥ Savannah Morning News Stories ᴥ

Any old news room is bound to have some great stories, but especially when the information center in question is located smack in the heart of downtown Savannah. The 1850 building—a site established for the purpose of informing the public (now being transformed into a hotel)—has its own stories to tell. Two great books have been written on the subject, which are listed at the end of this chapter.

There was the sports editor in the 1960's who suffered a massive heart attack and crumpled to the floor. Encountering the prone body, the city editor surveyed the scene coolly and remarked, "That'll be the last deadline he misses."

Sometimes the newsroom was the scene of strangeness as well. A witch doctor strolled into the newsroom one day, dressed in a long white robe and carrying an ornamented staff. He raised his arms and thundered (in a voice reminiscent of James Earl Jones): "WHERE IS DIANE SMITH?" The room fell silent. The aforementioned Diane was a police reporter who had done a story on the witch doctor being cited by the Savannah P.D. for killing a chicken and spilling its blood on the sidewalk. He then explained that the police had misidentified him. "My name is 'Baba', not 'Bubba'."

ᴥ The DeSoto Hotel ᴥ

The DeSoto Hotel once stood on the site of the present-day DeSoto Hilton, located at the corner of Bull and Liberty Streets. The opulent hotel was built in 1890, but was torn down in 1966 to make way for progress: the old building had no air conditioning. Many Savannahians bemoan the loss of the DeSoto, pointing to the Hilton and claiming that it has no character and that the architecture does not fit the city plan.

However, the former hotel is not forgotten. One story still told regarding the departed DeSoto is about a former prominent Savannah TV personality, who goes unnamed for reasons which will soon be clear to all. It seems this minor Savannah celebrity would often rent a room at the DeSoto to work the kinks out, so to speak. This fellow was married, with children, and had a television program that projected a wholesome image, but he would engage in the following ritual: he would rent his usual room in normal clothes, and then change into ladies apparel and lead a whole new life unknown to his fans and family. This continued for years, and apparently the outfit he wore was so radically different from his normal appearance that no one in the lobby put two and two together, namely that he and this 'lady' were in fact the same person. In fact, the outfit was quite convincing, and most never realized that she was a he.

The problem, however, was that one night this TV personality was coming back to the hotel in full costume with a young gentleman in tow, when 'she' suddenly realized that the keys had inadvertently been locked inside the room. To the TV personality's utter embarrassment, he had to go down to the lobby's front desk and ask to be let into 'Mr. So-and-So's' room. The clerk, still not realizing that he was in fact talking to this prominent citizen dressed in drag, asked if the 'woman' had any identification. The fellow had no other option other than to reveal his true colors by pulling off the wig. The man's TV program, understandably, was cancelled shortly thereafter.

Rebecca Clark also told an anecdote about the former bar, the Sapphire Room, at the old DeSoto Hotel. The owners installed a blacklight at the entrance to give it more of a classy look, but the vibe turned more 'upskirt' than 'upscale' when the blacklight began to seemingly undress the ladies walking into the establishment. The naked bulb lasted only a few days.

❧Reynolds Square a Crematorium?☙

An erroneous story that is often told as fact is that the townspeople were burning bodies of Yellow Fever epidemic victims in Reynolds Square (some name Johnson Square as the location). There is no documented evidence naming Reynolds Square, or any area of pre-1900's Savannah for that matter, as a crematorium.

The first problem with the claim that Reynolds Square was a crematorium is one of historical context. The practice of cremation was viewed as taboo in the Protestant, Catholic and Jewish religions until nearly 1900. Jews burned criminals, and the memory of burning heretics was so strong in the psyche of most Anglican-based religions that burning bodies, live or dead, would be seen as a punishment.

If bodies were going to be burned in Savannah, one would think that the city fathers would find a less public place to do the burning than Reynolds Square. This is, after all, the same square that housed the Silk Filature House, the home of James Habersham Jr., the Royal Council House and John Wesley's parsonage. The idea of mass-immolation in front of such structures, both because of the symbolism and the smell, is unlikely at best.

Add to that the problem of destroying a body by fire. It sounds easy, when in fact it is anything but. Nothing short of a coal furnace would be effective at destroying a body by fire. Also discounting this assertion is that building a bonfire in the middle of a square would be to invite disaster: Savannahians feared large fires due to the obvious threat to their homes.

The truth of the matter is that the bodies of epidemic victims were buried in our cemeteries, as evinced by the large number of tombstones bearing the dates of epidemic years. There is in fact a mass grave within Colonial Park Cemetery attributed to the Yellow Fever epidemic of 1820, and many graves of Yellow Fever victims in both Laurel Grove and Bonaventure Cemetery.

❧Sherman's Troops & Foraging Follies☙

This country will be drenched in blood... Oh, it is all folly, madness, a crime against civilization. You people speak so lightly of war. You don't know what you are talking about. War is a terrible thing.

You mistake, too, the people of the North... you are rushing into war with one of the most powerful, ingeniously mechanical, and determined people on earth right at your doors. You are bound to fail.

-William Tecumseh Sherman,
speaking to Southern friends when South Carolina seceded from the Union

Sherman's troops, in their 1864 March to the Sea, were raiding the plantations from Atlanta all the way to Savannah, and what they couldn't steal, they burned. The Southern families would often try to hide their valuables by either burying them, or concealing them in the family burial plot or vault, hoping the Union troops would be squeamish about violating their dead. Of course, after a while the first place the Bluecoats would look was the graves of the plantation.

Sherman's troops did manage to forage successfully, but not without some hitches. The Union troops quickly learned that Georgians were burying their valuables, and on one property discovered freshly dug ground. Figuring it to be treasure, the soldiers reached for their shovels, over the protests of the family. The men got very excited when they struck a small pine box, but when the lid was lifted they caught a whiff of a ghastly odor. In the box was a cocker spaniel, very deceased. "Looks like poor Curly will get no peace. That's the fourth time he's been dug up today," lamented one of the family members.

✎Stairing, Staring, and Embarrassing✎

When Savannah College of Art and Design (SCAD) bought the old Levy's Department Store Building, they sought to turn the 1950's-era structure into their new library. Located at the corner of Abercorn and Broughton streets, the Art Deco building now houses the Jen Library, which opened in the mid-1990's.

Those at SCAD overseeing the renovation of the old Levy Building wanted to do something unusual for their planned state-of-the-art facility, and plans were drawn up to build a staircase out of glass—where the actual steps one walked on would be made of that unorthodox building material. Constructing it proved to be successful. The implementation of the new stairs, however, could have used a bit more thought.

As soon as the library opened, the stairs drew a lot of attention. The layout of the library had even situated couches and chairs *under* the stairs, to highlight the achievement, and the couches seemed to be always occupied—by male students. It was only then that members of the staff began to question the wisdom of this arrangement: the students congregating under the staircase were viewing more than reading material, and the wonderful engineering feat was revealing more than just an architect's skill. To put it simply, the boys could look up more than just books in the Jen Library—and it was a revealing moment for the student body.

Red-faced administrators ordered the staircase to be disassembled, and one side each of the glass stairs was frosted to prevent any more voyeurism.

☞Crime & Punishment☜

Early in the colony's history, there was no formal law. A listing of the crimes that the first settlers on the Georgia committed under English common law sometimes reveals some interesting or humorous instances. Even within landing on the site of our present-day city in 1733, James Edward Oglethorpe had to deal with some bizarre circumstances. A servant girl of one of the passengers was accused of "loose disorderly behavior," apparently attempting to seduce several other young women. She was sentenced to be tied to a cart and dragged throughout the settlement—which does not sound quite like the roll in the hay the servant maid had envisioned. Oglethorpe remitted her punishment and sent her to Charleston.

But there are others: consider the case of Mary Preston, who came to Savannah aboard the *Georgia Pink*. She was accused of picking the pockets of a fellow passenger, a man who happened to be very intoxicated. Her defense was that she was also very intoxicated, and unaware of what she had done.

And then there was the case of Elizabeth Malpas, whose name in French literally translates as 'bad step'. Elizabeth was tried and found guilty of "lyeing between two fellows naked & leading a dissolute life." She was whipped and dragged up and down Bull Street.

Not all crimes were punished: Patrick Tailfer was a farmer until thirteen of his eighteen servants fled his 'care', apparently to escape their cruel master. Tailfer also seduced one young girl and wound up selling her to the Indians. He also beat one of his servants to death, a move that probably precipitated the mutiny. Unbelievably, Tailfer switched professions and became, of all things, a *physician*.

⌖Further Reading⌖

If this small sampling of true tales does not sate the hunger for all things Savannah, I suggest reading *Savannah Lore and More*, by Tom Coffey, and *Behind the Moss Curtain*, by Murray Silver.

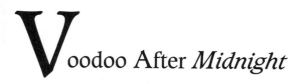

Voodoo After *Midnight*

Questions are frequently asked about the bestselling book *Midnight in the Garden of Good and Evil*. The book, purported to be non-fiction, details the death of a young man at the hands of one of the most prominent men in Savannah society, antiques dealer Jim Williams, who claimed self-defense. The novel documents the May 2nd, 1981 slaying at the Mercer House, as well as the protracted trial's impact on Savannah's high-society.

Generally, this author is resistant to discussing the happenings within *Midnight*'s pages, for a number of reasons. Primarily because while the subject matter of the book is entertaining reading, it does not represent or bear much relation to the Savannah I know and love. One story, however which I will tell, however, which does relate indirectly to *Midnight* is one which explores the strange and unique side of Savannah's ties with the voodoo culture. For the very first time anywhere, this tale will see print within this volume.

One other reason I include this story is personal; to attempt to right what I perceive as a wrong characterization within *Midnight's* pages. I make no accusations towards the talented author of the aforementioned book, Mr. John Berendt. I simply disagree with his portrayal of the late Judge George Oliver, who presided over the courtroom case Berendt chronicled in his book. Judge Oliver, who will henceforth be called 'Judge', was made to look old, tired, and uncaring in the book. In one passage it is hinted that he fell asleep while court was in session. This in no way describes the man that I met on a handful of occasions. Old, yes; but the Judge was always sharp as a tack, quick-witted, and full of vigor.

I found myself sitting next to the Judge and his charming wife during Thanksgiving, 1994. Of course, I had already read *Midnight*, which had just been released, and was fascinated. I had been invited to dinner by Miss Helen, who was the mother of a client for whom I had painted a mural. Miss Helen, who spoke with a nearly indecipherable Greek accent when it suited her not to be understood, and near flawless English the rest of the time, had heard that I would be unable to go home for Thanksgiving. Her famous Greek hospitality wouldn't stand for me sitting at my apartment alone during the Holiday, which is how I wound up sitting next to the Judge with a plateful of turkey.

I had wondered the identity of the gentleman sitting to my right who regaled us with story after side-splitting story, mostly involving the Savannah elite. When I asked Miss Helen, who had come close to me while serving gravy, she turned on the Greek accent. "That's the Judge, dear," she said, and when I asked her if it was the judge from *Midnight*, she confirmed this. I was suddenly full of questions regarding the famous case, but Miss Helen read my mind. "Don't you dare," she hissed. "Wait... until he has a few drinks in him." I took from this that it was a sore subject with the Judge.

I, of course, did exactly as I was told. One did not quibble with Miss Helen's instructions. I waited until the Judge looked well-warmed, shall we say, and I looked to Miss Helen, who gave me a nearly imperceptible nod, meaning, *go ahead.* I leaned over and asked him timidly about the story. My question dealt with the fact that he had heard all the facts of the case, and in fact was the very one who ruled whether something could be entered as evidence, and was thus in a unique position to say whether Williams was innocent or guilty.

He turned to face me, and the room went absolutely quiet. He took a long time in answering.

"You want to know if Jim Williams did it, do you?" I suddenly knew why the man had been a successful judge for so long: when he needed to be, Judge Oliver could be incredibly intimidating. I can only imagine the power he held over witnesses, juries and even lawyers. Then the Judge's features softened. "Oh yes. That son of a gun Jim Williams was absolutely guilty of cold-blooded murder."

The room seemed stunned. "I'll tell you another thing, too. *I do not blame him.* That boy he shot was trouble with a capital 'T', and the only one who couldn't see that was Williams." The Judge moved to stand up, and added, "Sometimes, people just need killing." And with that, the Judge left the room.

✍A Terrifying Aftermath of *Midnight* ✍

It was while he was out of the room that his wife told a story of her own indirectly related to *Midnight*. After the case was over, all that her and her husband wanted was to be left alone. They refused interviews, including several requests by John Berendt. She prefaced the story by saying that they had never told this story to anyone, but it had been on her mind lately.

"After the case was over, we left Savannah and went out to our vacation spot on Tybee just to get away. The political climate was so hot in Savannah that we just couldn't stay. So we locked up the house, set the new security system, and took a little break for a while.

"Upon returning, we noticed something odd. The security alarm was still set, but some things had been moved ever so slightly in the house. Nothing was missing as far as we could tell, but we kept finding dirt in the house even though it had been thoroughly cleaned before we left. We also found this white powder, like talcum powder, in a few spots. We didn't think that much about it, until we restocked the refrigerator.

Inside the butter dish, feet-up, was a dead bird."

I did not understand—I hadn't been in Savannah long enough to know what that meant. So I asked her how that could be.

"Young man, you don't really think that little bird let itself into our house, flew to the fridge and opened it, opened up the dairy case door, and crawled under the butter cover to die, do you? That dead bird was voodoo, dear." When I asked what she and her husband did then, she said, "Well, we cleaned it up and got a new security system. We couldn't do much else about it, could we?"

That was when Miss Helen piped in, "You could have always moved... I might've."

Ron Higgins & the Liberty City House

Ron Higgins, known as "Hollywoood" to most locals, was many things in his lifetime: tour guide, business owner, entrepreneur, sports fan, lover of great food, consummate prankster, and one of my best friends. He was a classic example of what Malcom Gladwell described as "Connector" in his seminal book about marketing: *The Tipping Point: How Little Things Can Make a Big Difference.* A "Connector", as described by Gladwell, is a touchtone for the community and flashpoint for ideas, two traits Ron certainly embodied for we Savannahians. It seems like everyone in town knew 'Hollywood' Ron, and he never met a stranger. Which is why it pains me so much to type these words: Ron Higgins passed away in the summer of 2010. He was only 45 years young.

It was the act of compiling this volume that really introduced me to Ron, so in a strange sense this book you're holding in your hands is responsible for the very friendship I'm describing. I was researching ghost stories, and writing down locals' true accounts of their own encounters with the supernatural. I had no idea how long the book would take to complete, or even if it would be published when I was finished. It was just a subject for which I had a passion, and Ron was likewise fascinated with ghost stories. I spoke to Ron regarding my little project and he intimated that he grew up in a haunted house, which is a shared experience for many Savannahians. We sat down for lunch together, and he told me the whole story.

"In 1979, I lived in Liberty City," he began. Liberty City, it must be explained, is actually not a city at all but a section of midtown Savannah about a mile and a half from the Historic District. "I was trying to get to sleep in my bedroom, but the pull handles on my dresser kept clicking. I thought it was the central heat rattling the house, so I lay there and listened to the clicking. Suddenly I realized that the central heat had turned off, and the handles were still clicking at a pretty good clip. Nothing else in the room was vibrating, but the handles were rattling.

"I have always had a thing about counting to thirteen when I'm nervous or scared—it's my favorite number. Well, this scared me—I was pretty young at this point. I counted to thirteen in my head, hoping it would stop, but it didn't. When I finally reached that number and the dresser was still rattling, I leaped out of bed and tried to run. The funny thing was, I was in socks on hardwood, so I slipped and wound up doing a split right there in my room. I scrambled up to my feet and ran as fast as I could."

Ron went on to say that it was not an isolated case. There was an incident that his entire family witnessed one night when the power went out. His brother heard a strange sound coming from the kitchen. "A rattling sound was coming from near the refrigerator, which is odd when you consider there was no power. So my brother goes in there with a flashlight, and suddenly he yells out for us to come there. When we get into the kitchen, he trains the flashlight on a plate which is on the counter between the sink and the fridge, and there are pieces of silverware on the plate jumping around on top of the plate! Nothing else in the kitchen was rattling or vibrating, just the utensils on the plate. And remember, the power is out. My whole family saw this."

Ron also had a strange experience one night in 1996. He was resting on the bed one night, lying on his side facing the wall. He suddenly felt a pressure pushing him down into the mattress. "I thought it was my sister, just kidding around. It felt like a hand pushing me straight down, so I turned my head—and there was no one there."

Hollywood Ron's experiences with the supernatural, while they may seem out of the ordinary to outsiders, often times will produce a nod of the head and a smile in a Savannahian. Whether it is an encounter with a phantom or apparition, a problem with poltergeists, or a vision of a departed loved one, most conversations with a longtime resident or native will inevitably turn to the supernatural.

Is it possible that Ron's supernatural experiences don't end with his much-too-soon death? Is this in fact not a passing, but instead a new begining for a man who was constantly reinventing himself? And more importantly, is it possible to be "pranked" from beyond the grave?

One night while I was leading a tour, a lone woman on the pub crawl approached me, but seemed unsure if she should say what was on her mind. After I reassured her, she said, "Did you have a friend pass away recently?" This conversation occured about two weeks after Ron had passed away. I told her yes.

"Was he a... big fella?" Again, I answered yes, that my friend who had passed away was pretty tall and was a former football player.

"Was his name either 'Ron' or 'John'?" At this, I'm sure I went dreadfully pale.

The woman placed her arm on me. "I have the ability to 'see' or 'hear' things, sometimes, that other people can't. Do you understand?" I answered her in the affirmative, between stiff lips. "Well," she continued, "Ron has been following you around all night."

"Does he...does he have a message for me?" I asked.

"I asked him that very question, and he said no, he just wanted to mess with you!"

Ron Higgins owned 'Savannah Movie Tours', which tours film locations used in major motion pictures throughout Savannah's beautiful Historic District. Hollywood Ron was involved in the production of many award winning films, including Training Day, Amistad, Pearl Harbor, Remember the Titans, Armageddon and Sweet Home Alabama. The tours still continue on, year round. For reservations please call (877) 444-FILM, or (912) 234-3440.

www.savannahmovietours.com.

Fort Pulaski

In the War for American Independence, the Allies' misguided assault ranks among the most costly and bloody hour of the entire conflict. Among the dead was Polish Count Casimir Pulaski, who was the highest-ranking foreign officer to die in the Revolution. He was called the Father of the American Cavalry, and he served as George Washington's personal bodyguard. But the dashing officer died as so many men did in the futile charge against well-entrenched British positions.

Ft. Pulaski, named for the brave and bold Count, was designed in part by Robert E. Lee, back when he was fresh out of West Point, in 1831. The future commander of the Army of Northern Virginia in the Civil War, Lee was in charge of sorting out the complex task of drainage of the swamp on which the fort now sits. Pulaski was designed to be an impregnable fortress, with masonry walls seven and a half feet thick. It was seized by the Confederates nearly three months before the attack on Ft. Sumter, so the taking of the fort was actually the first military action of the Civil War.

The fort was well-fortified, having fifty cannon, when the Union landed on Tybee Island very late in 1861. The Union spent months sneaking their own cannon onto Tybee, working at night as to not draw fire from the fort. The guns which the Union was hard at work concealing consisted of a new type of cannon, which was untested in combat. The rifled cannon could fire shells further than ever before, but of even more importance was their accuracy. The Rebels defending the fort were unaware of the existence of this new weapon, and were not terribly concerned about the Union soldiers on Tybee Island, because they appeared to be too far away to be able to cause serious damage to the fort.

Military wisdom held that cannon were ineffective against stone or masonry forts at a range of 800 or more yards—and the Union artillery was more than twice that distance away. The Rebels were well-trained, and had enough provisions and powder to withstand a siege of 4 months or more. Their commander, Col. Charles Olmstead, was arguably the best artillerist in the Confederacy. He personally aimed a shot at two Union soldiers who had walked out onto the beach to taunt the Confederates—*and the cannonball cut one of the soldiers in half*. The Union soldiers learned a quick lesson not to taunt the Confederate gunners.

Thirty-six Union guns squared off against fifty on the Confederate side. The battle began on April 10th, 1862. Confederate General John Pemberton, watching the battle, suggested that Fort Pulaski was wasting shot and powder by returning fire against the Union attack, because after all, wasn't the fort impregnable?

The rifled Union guns proved to be far more effective than anyone imagined. Their incredible accuracy at long-range began to take a toll on the fort's southeast wall. The guns kept up their pounding of Ft. Pulaski through that night, and in the morning of the 11th it became apparent that the fort's integrity had been compromised. By noon, a gaping hole had been blasted through one wall in the fort, and Union shells were entering the fort itself. These shots were hitting the wall of the powder magazine, which contained forty thousand pounds (twenty tons) of gunpowder. Col. Olmstead was faced with a terrible choice: surrender, or see both himself and his men killed in a massive explosion. Olmstead, upon surrendering, said, "I yield my sword. I trust I have not disgraced it."

Fort Pulaski, the supposedly impregnable fortress, surrendered after thirty hours of shelling. The immovable object met the irresistible force, and the results were disastrous for the Confederacy. Col. Olmstead and his men spent most of the remainder of the war in Union prisons.

৫৯ 'The Immortal Six Hundred' ৹৯

But the truly terrible had yet to occur. It wasn't until 1864 that six hundred captured Confederate officers were interred at the former Rebel stronghold by the Union Army. These men became pawns in a war of retribution between the two sides—a disagreement over the proper treatment and housing of prisoners of war. These men, called "The Immortal Six Hundred", were placed on starvation rations to retaliate for the barbaric practice of the Confederates of placing Union P.O.W.'s in the line of fire to protect vital interests, essentially using them as human shields.

These six hundred men were forced to survive by eating rats, cats, and in one case, a kitten. One of these cats belonged to the daughter of the Union camp commander. Forty-four of these men died as a direct result of their treatment, be it the harsh and unheated quarters or the lack of nutrients. Thirteen of them were buried in unmarked graves somewhere in or around Fort Pulaski. But even the ones who survived continued to have health problems years later in spite of their release.

As late as 1930, one survivor was still bitter. He was quoted in an interview as saying that while he loved his country. It was still a thrill to see the flag, "but with that thrill comes an unspeakable sadness; for it was the Stars and Stripes that floated over... Pulaski."

৫৯ Parade Ground Happenings ৹৯

Numerous people have reported seeing or experiencing strange things at Fort Pulaski. One couple reported seeing a soldier atop the parapet near dusk. "He was standing at the edge, wearing a dark blue jacket," the woman remembers, "and then he simply stepped back out of view. I walked back, to get a better view of him, but he was gone." The man, a Civil War reenactor, confirmed this, but did add, "I don't think he was wearing blue. His jacket was definitely dark, but I know that some Confederate units wore a darker shade of gray than the others. It was a color called Richmond Gray—it was almost black, it was so dark—and they called it that because it was issued at a depot located in Richmond, Virginia." Then perhaps to assuage the stormy look his wife gave him, he added: "In the dim light of the setting sun, it probably did look blue to Sharon, but I'm certain it was Richmond Gray because I have just such an outfit at home. The fellow was wearing wooden buttons—he was Confederate."

There are living historian interpreters in the fort from time to time who do in fact dress from that time period, but given the acrimony even today over the Union occupation of Pulaski, it would be unlikely that any of the reenactors would wear blue. But it does bear pointing out that Fort Pulaski was only under Confederate control for one year in the conflict, so if they did in fact see the spirit of a departed soldier, he would be much more likely to be wearing blue.

Another man visiting the fort reported hearing strange sounds in the powder magazine. "I was viewing the display, and I distinctly heard someone say, 'Charlie, come here.' I stepped out into the parade ground and there was no one there. It sounded like he was right there at my shoulder when he spoke, but I could see no one around me."

Others, including this author, have felt something amiss in the soldier's quarters. I attended a reenactment entitled "Christmas with the Troops" in 2002. Along with firing the cannon and doing parade ground exercises, the well-drilled reenactors (and period-costumed ladies) also provided ginger cookies and some good cider around a roaring fire, where we sang traditional holiday folk songs. It was midway through singing that I began to feel ill. I experienced a claustrophobic despair unlike any I've ever felt. My whole body began tingling, and I had to step outside. I leaned on a brick archway and tried to regain my composure, and one of the older reenactors walked over to check on me. "Feeling okay, young fella?" He asked. I told him I needed air, and added that I had never had an anxiety attack before and had never experienced claustrophobia, either. He smiled grimly, and said, "You're not the first. Given the history of that area you were just standing, it isn't a shock at all. It happens all the time—people feel sick, and once they get outside they feel fine."

It is not surprising that an area so imbued with turmoil and despair would be haunted. Both the terrific pounding absorbed by the fort in those desperate hours of early 1862, and the confinement of the Immortal Six Hundred in 1864 could well have seeped into the very brick walls of the fortification. The anguish of both events cannot help but have repercussions even today.

Fort Screven Inn

On Tybee Island near North Beach sits a fortification called Fort Screven, built in 1897. It was constructed to bolster the coastal defenses and defend the mouth of the Savannah River during the Spanish-American War, and served that purpose until after the Second World War. Also part of the Ft. Screven complex was the old hospital complex, a collection of houses just a few hundred yards to the south of the main fortification. Those buildings have been turned into private residences in some cases, but also into a popular bed & breakfast, which is named for the fort. But the Ft. Screven Inn has another reputation other than beautiful rooms and friendly staff, with unexplainable and sometimes terrifying results.

This story takes on personal significance to this author, because I worked and lived at the Inn during the winter and spring of 1997. I did not believe in ghosts when I began the job, but by the end of my stay I was very much a believer in the supernatural. I was hired originally to be the caretaker just during the winter months for a friend's bed & breakfast, but I was requested to stay on for some additional time when the owner returned.

When I was interviewing for the position, I remember being asked whether or not I believed in ghosts. My response was an emphatic 'no'. With that, my friend was satisfied, but added that he had previously had a hard time keeping innkeepers around because of all the spectral activity. After showing me the ropes of the job for a few days, he departed for Texas for several weeks.

A Non-Believer is Converted

Early on in my stay, I began to notice that there were some strange sounds originating in the hallway. The sounds were like someone was walking up and down the hall with heavy boots—but there was no one there. This happened at all hours of the day and night. I at first attributed this to the settling and groaning of an old house. It was, after all, built on a hill which sloped back with the property, and the winter months on Tybee can be pretty windy. One guest complained about the person stomping out in the hallway in the middle of the night, but the inn was empty except for that couple and me, and I didn't leave my room all evening.

The incident that really changed my mind about the reality of ghosts also involved the hallway, specifically the door leading down to the basement. Often times in the course of my daily routine, I would walk past and find the door unlocked. It was one of those types of surface-bolt locking mechanisms, the type where a tubular bolt on the door slides into a corresponding clasp on the doorframe, and some days the door would be unlocked nearly every time I'd walk by. It seemed to be more likely to happen when I was all alone in the inn. On one occasion, I locked it, and turned around to walk down the hall, and I heard it unlock behind me! I heard the distinctive *click* of the tubular bolt sliding to the open position. I turned back, and sure enough, the door was unlocked again.

I started to think that maybe the hallway was warped or had settled, and perhaps the force exerted by the shifting weight of walking down the hallway could explain why it was unlocking. So I walked backwards down the hall, watching the bolt the whole time—and nothing. It didn't move. I even jumped up and down in that hall, I'm sure it was quite a sight. I reached out to see if it was loosened, and my fingers got within a couple of inches, and *the lock unlocked by itself.* The door then opened by itself. I saw it happen with my own eyes. Needless to say, I didn't go anywhere near that door for a while.

When my friend returned from Texas, the first question he asked me was, "Do you believe in ghosts now?" I had to admit yes. After so many unexplainable things happened to me, I began to accept that there are other forces at work that we simply do not understand. That door in particular was an area where many, many baffling events took place. On another occasion, the door itself was pounded with a knocking so loud that I heard the commotion from where I was sitting outside, on the front porch swing. I rushed to the hallway to see what the matter was, and the door was once again slowly opening by itself.

ᴄᴏFrightening Twistsᴄᴏ

On a few occasions, the strange happenings took a scary turn. One guest left abruptly early one morning, complaining that someone unseen had held her down in bed and bitten her on the side of the neck. She did have a red mark on the side of her neck that looked like teeth marks. She paid for her room in full, and practically ran to her car to get away from whatever she had encountered.

They were not the only guests to have an incident. A couple claimed that they experienced some very strange things one night. The young pair was awakened by a strange sound coming from the bedside table in their room. It was a strange vibrating sound, almost a ringing, as they described it. The couple noticed that not only was the racket coming from one of the bedside lamps, the lamp itself was also levitating ever so slightly, about a quarter of an inch. When the man reached over and touched it, he claimed the lamp dropped back down onto the table. Then the strange noise moved across the room and began to vibrate the TV. The most surprising part of this story is that the guests were not the least bit alarmed by this activity. They were laughing and joking the next morning at breakfast. The other guests loved it. When I asked them if they were disturbed or wanted to switch rooms, they both laughed harder and told me that they had both grown up in a haunted houses. They were a bit upset that the next night was perfectly peaceful. They were looking forward to another haunting!

I, as well as other guests, experienced a cold spot in one of the bedrooms. It felt as if the temperature dropped twenty degrees when you'd get near one side of the room. The air conditioner wasn't in use yet because it was still cool, and there was no draft in the room, but that spot was usually colder than the rest of the house for no discernable reason.

The ghost also was not without a sense of humor. A gruff guest named Ron who was combative with the staff and surly with his fellow guests suddenly accused first some other guests, and then me, of stealing his breakfast bagel from the freezer. A denial of this was insufficient, and the entire inn was searched for Ron's bagel, including the trash can—Ron was looking for evidence of the wrapper, which he thought would be proof that someone had eaten the breakfast roll. No bagel or wrapper turned up. Days after Ron and his wife departed the inn, the bagel suddenly surfaced, appearing right in plain view in the very front of the freezer. This became known jokingly by staff and guest alike as the 'Saga of Ron's Haunted Bagel'.

One afternoon I restocked the refrigerator with cans of soda that we provided for the guests. I walked back to the kitchen and put the remaining eight of the twelve-pack of sodas in the pantry, which is located right next to the main hallway. I placed the sodas on the center shelf, with the open end pointing up in the air. Now, this case of sodas was not near the edge of the shelf, and wasn't resting at an odd angle, or anything out of the ordinary. I walked away, and heard a bang that was so loud I jumped in the air. It really startled me. When I walked back to the kitchen to see what caused it, I found six of those soda cans rolling across the kitchen floor, all in a row, slowly rolling away from the pantry door. Two things about this still make me scratch my head even today: first, the cardboard case of sodas *was still upright in the pantry.* Did they jump out? Or did the case tip over and then somehow tip back with two soda cans still inside? Either way it's impossible. And the second really odd thing about it was the fact that the house had settled on its foundation, and the house was built on a hill that sloped back. *So when I found those Cokes rolling across the kitchen floor, they were rolling uphill.* I retreated out of the kitchen and didn't come back in for a while—I remember thinking that if something that odd was going to be happening in there, I wanted to be nowhere near it. That was one of the strangest experiences of my life.

On one occasion where I was downstairs in the basement, I saw something out of the corner of my eye. When I turned around to see what it was, I realized that the pull-chains attached to the electric lights were all swaying back and forth, as if someone had batted them all at once. On another, also in the basement, the lights went out on me even though the light switch was at the top of the stairs and the door had not opened. In the absolute dark I made my way back to the top of the stairs and found the light switch in the 'off' position. No one else was even staying in the Inn—I was all alone.

The strangeness was not just experienced by humans. One couple who stayed at the inn had a dog that apparently did not like the main hallway. It would cry and whine, wanting either to go into the room they had rented, or back outside. And not just dogs sensed something unusual. We took in two kittens that had been found near the Inn, and on several occasions I noticed that they would both watch something that only they could see. They would both be fixated on the same invisible object, eyes and heads turning in unison.

Another innkeeper who worked around the same time period stayed in the upstairs. She was uncomfortable in her room, even with all the lights on. She claims that she often felt the sensation of being watched while she was watching television. "One night I was sitting on the bed, and I kept being distracted from the program by the feeling of a presence in the room... coldness, and an uncomfortable scrutiny. I kept turning my head quickly, to see if I could catch sight of whoever was with me, but I never saw anyone in the room when I tried to catch them that way. But once, rather than turn my head towards the right, which is where I kept feeling the presence, I turned my head instead to the left, toward the mirror. I saw a *man* in the mirror, and he was standing right next to the bed—and right next to me! I screamed and ran out of the room. That was my last night in the inn. I told the management that they could keep the job, because I had had enough." She described the man as wearing a uniform that had a military cut, light greenish-tan in color, and a wide-brimmed hat.

Both that former innkeeper and I were in total agreement when asked about the frequency of strange occurrences. "I'd say that things happened almost daily," she said.

Some activity also centered on a certain candlestick holder attached to the wall in the main front room— occasionally it would be found upside down in the mornings, and it wasn't loose in its attachment to the wall. It took a degree of force to spin it upside down, and yet it was a common occurrence to find it inverted.

Call From the Other Side?

A mother and daughter who stayed at the inn had what was perhaps a call from the other side late one September night in 2001. Resting peacefully in their room, the phone rang, waking them both. The mother picked up the receiver, and heard a strange static sound, so she hung up. One they fell asleep, the phone rang again, with the same result. The older woman looked for a ringer on the phone so she could turn it off, but found none. When it rang a third time, the daughter picked up the phone and a strange male voice said, "Tell Emily I'm sorry for waking her up," and the line went dead. Emily was indeed the name of the mother, so the pair assumed the caller had been one of the other guests staying at the inn that night whom they had met earlier that evening, and they had made a mistake trying to dial out of the building.

The next morning at breakfast, the mother and daughter commented on the ringing phone. The owner of the inn pursed her lips and said, "Someone called your room last night? That's impossible. It has to be patched through to your room from downstairs, and no one was awake to transfer your call. Also, that phone can't ring. There's no ringer inside it—we have to knock on your door for you to know someone is calling." Not batting an eyelash, the daughter said, "Well, at least the ghost was polite!" This drew a laugh from guests and staff alike.

The current owners are not believers in ghosts. But when asked about unexplained happenings at the inn, one of the owners said, "I don't believe in this paranormal stuff at all. But my mother, who is a believer, worked here for a short time. She was so uncomfortable in this house she moved back to Atlanta, and she claimed it was because she could feel a presence here."

And what of the identity of the ghost or ghosts? There are several possible explanations. The house, as previously mentioned, was part of the hospital complex. It was also one of the few buildings associated with the fort which had a basement. One of the former owners claims that bodies of men in the fort who died in accidents were stored downstairs. Another possible source would be the twenty-plus years the building served as a nursing home. So there is a possibility that the ghost is a serviceman who died in the hospital portion of the structure, but there is also a possibility that the undeparted spirit could have ties to the period of time when the house became a nursing home. Either way, the house has associations with death. Fortunately, neither the nonliving nor the living seems to mind sharing such a beautiful bed and breakfast.

Savannah's Squares: A Haunted Guide

Franklin Square, laid out in 1791 to honor Benjamin Franklin, was known as 'Water Tower' or 'Reservoir' Square. Located on this square is the First African Baptist Church, the first African-American church in America. The square was lost in the 1960's, with Montgomery Street running straight through it, but it has since been restored. Haunted sites near Franklin Square include B & B Billiards, located on Congress St., and the Scarbrough House.

Ellis Square, one of the original squares laid out in 1733, honors Royal Governor Henry Ellis. For years the square was a public market in various forms. In 1954 the historic marketplace that encompassed the lot was razed to make way for parking. It is undergoing massive restoration to house underground parking and a square at street level.

Johnson Square, which was the first square in 1733, honors Robert Johnson, the Royal Governor of South Carolina. This square was the site of the Trustees' public store and bread mill and oven. Christ Episcopal Church stands on the southeastern trust lot. This is the site of the first church in Georgia, first holding services in 1733. The current structure was built in 1840. A monument to Revolutionary War hero Nathanael Greene is located in the center of Johnson Square, and was erected in 1829. Today the square is known by many residents simply as 'Banking Square' because of the many financial institutions located here. Haunted sites around Johnson Square include the former Pulaski Hotel, which is currently a bank.

Reynolds Square was laid out in 1733, and was named for Captain John Reynolds, our first Royal Governor. This square was formerly the site of the filature house, where silk was produced, and the Royal Council House. The Habersham House, built in 1771, still stands today as the Olde Pink House Restaurant. Located on Abercorn Street on the southeast corner of the square is the Lucas Theatre, which was built in 1921. The monument in the center of the square is honoring John Wesley, the founder of Methodism. Haunted sites located on Reynolds Square include the Olde Pink House, the Lucas Theatre, and the Planters Inn.

Warren Square was laid out in 1791, and honors General Joseph Warren, who died at Bunker Hill. Haunted sites near Warren Square include B. Matthews Bakery & Eatery on Bay St.

Washington Square was laid out in 1791, and honors the first United States President, George Washington. Around both Washington and Warren Square are some of the oldest wooden structures in the city, with most dating from the 18ᵗʰ century. Haunted sites located near Washington Square include the Hampton Lillibridge House, the Mulberry Inn, the Pirate's House, and Trustees Garden.

Liberty Square was laid out in 1799. It honors the Liberty Boys, who were the local branch of the resistance during the American Revolution. The square was lost when it was paved through for an Interstate 16 interchange. On one remaining bit of the square there is a Flame of Freedom monument.

Telfair Square was established in 1733, and honors former Governor Edward Telfair. The square was originally named St. James, for the royal residence in London. Located on the square are the Telfair Museum of Art, which was originally Gov. Telfair's mansion, and also the Trinity United Methodist Church.

Wright Square was laid out in 1733, and honors Sir James Wright, 3ʳᵈ and last Royal Governor. Located on the square are the Old Courthouse building, and the Lutheran Church of the Ascension. Monuments are a marker to William Washington Gordon, and a Tomochichi monument. Haunted sites near Wright Square include 12 West Oglethorpe Ave.

Oglethorpe Square was laid out in 1742 to honor James Edward Oglethorpe. Located on the square are the Richardson-Owens-Thomas House, the Cluskey Building, and a marker for the Moravian colonists. Haunted sites located near Oglethorpe Square include the Owens-Thomas House.

Columbia Square was established in 1799 to honor the female personification of the United States. Located on the square are the Kehoe House, the Davenport House, and the Wormsloe Fountain. Haunted sites located near Columbia Square include the 17Hundred90 Inn & Restaurant, the Kehoe House, and the Davenport House.

Greene Square, laid out in 1799, honors General Nathanael Greene of Revolutionary War fame. Located on the square is the Second African Baptist Church. Haunted sites located near Greene Square include a former orphanage which has been converted to a residential dwelling.

Elbert Square, which was laid out in 1801, honors Revolutionary War hero Samuel Elbert. This square was lost when it was paved through for an Interstate 16 interchange. Only a small strip of grass remains next to the Civic Center.

Orleans Square, laid out in 1815 to honor the American victory at the Battle of New Orleans. Located on the square are the Champion-McAlpin House and the German Memorial Fountain.

Chippewa Square was laid out in 1815 in honor of the American victory at the Battle of Chippewa. Located on the square are the First Baptist Church, the Savannah Theatre, and a monument to James Edward Oglethorpe. Also notable was the filming of the 'bench scene' in *Forrest Gump* at the northernmost point of the square. Haunted sites located near Chippewa Square include the Savannah Theatre, and McDonough's Restaurant & Lounge.

Crawford Square was laid out in 1841 to honor Secretary of the Treasury William Harris Crawford.

Pulaski Square was laid out in 1837 to honor Count Casimir Pulaski, the highest-ranking foreign officer to die in the American Revolution.

Madison Square, established in 1837, honors James Madison, the 4th President of the United States. Located on the square are the Green Meldrim House, the Sorrel-Weed House, St. John's Episcopal Church, and the Savannah Volunteer Guards Armory. Also located on Madison Square are monuments to Revolutionary War hero Sergeant William Jasper and a monument marking the southernmost point of British lines during the Siege of Savannah.

Lafayette Square was established in 1837 to honor the Marquis de Lafayette. Located on the square are the Andrew Low House, the Hamilton-Turner Mansion, the Cathedral of St. John the Baptist, and Flannery O'Connor's childhood home. In the center of the square is a fountain erected by the Colonial Dames. Haunted sites located near Lafayette Square include the Andrew Low House, 215 East Charlton St., and the Hamilton-Turner Mansion.

Troup Square, laid out in 1851, is named for Senator George Michael Troup. Located on the square are both the Unitarian Universalist Church and the Armillary Sphere.

Chatham Square, laid out in 1847, honors William Pitt, the Earl of Chatham.

Monterey Square was established in 1847, and named for a battle in the Mexican War. The Mercer House, the Temple Mickve Israel, and a monument to Revolutionary War hero Count Casimir Pulaski, highest ranking officer to die in the American Revolution, are all located on this square.

Calhoun Square, laid out in 1851, was named for John C. Calhoun, South Carolina United States Senator, Congressman and Vice President. Located on the square are the Massie School and Wesley Monumental United Methodist Church.

Whitefield Square was established in 1851, and honors Reverend George Whitefield, the founder of Bethesda Orphanage. Located on the square are the Congregational Church and a gazebo.

* Savannah Haunted History Tour, a Candlelight Walking Tour
Tours at 7 and 9 pm nightly
Depart from the front gates of Colonial Park Cemetery

* Savannah Spirits Haunted Pub Crawl
Tours: 8 pm nightly @ Moon River Brewing Company, 21 W. Bay St.
9 pm nightly @ Molly MacPherson's Pub, 311 W. Congress St.

Contact Cobblestone Tours at (912) 604-3007

OTHER TITLES BY BONAVENTTURE

When Elvis Meets the Dalai Lama
by Murray Silver

The author of *Great Balls of Fire: The Uncensored Story of Jerry Lee Lewis* recounts his favorite stories of how he started out as a rock concert promoter in the late 1960's and ended up as a special assistant to His Holiness the XIVth Dalai Lama. A magical mystery tour of pop culture spanning the 50's through the 90's, with anecdotes about Jerry Lee Lewis, Elvis Presley, professional wrestler Harley Race, pornographer Gail Palmer, and the Tibetan Buddhist monks of Drepung Loseling Monastery. Never before published photographs throughout!

Hardback, 384 pages. ISBN 978-0-9724224-4-4

Behind the Moss Curtain and Other Great Savannah Stories
by Murray Silver

Ten true stories not found anywhere else in print. Most of the stories are about the good old days when Savannah was run by gangsters and gamblers, a time when the town was known as the "Independent State of Chatham County." Some tragic, some comic, a few ghosts...but all true! The best book ever written about Savannah.

Hardback, 286 pages. ISBN 978-0-9724224-0-6

Fastened to the Marsh, A Savannah Saga
by Jan Durham

The story traces a family's legacy from arrival of an 18th century indentured servant to the begrudging return of her last legitimate descendant in the 21th century. Ten generations of stallwart women, illustrating family relationships, loyalty, caregiving, finding source of our strength.

Softback, 247 pages   ISBN 978-0-9724224-7-5

Spirit Willing, a Savannah Haunting
by Susan B. Johnson

A tale of conniving and greed in which Charlotte Horner exacts revenge by planning to oust her aging aunt from her historic Savannah home. Aunt Olivia obtains the unconventional alliance of her great great grandfather Cyrus, dead for 100 years, when all start to question her mental stability, even the lady herself. A splendid tale of Savannah's past that breaks through to the present!

Hardback, 230 pages. ISBN 978-0-9724224-6-8

Phantoms of History: Savannah DVD

Hunts for ghosts through the pages of history and compares haunted fiction with historic fact. By BRG productions and distributed by Bonaventture Books.

To order: Sales@Bonaventture.com

Tel or fax (912) 355-7054